Isavasya Upanishad

RAJ BHAMBU

NOTION PRESS

NOTION PRESS

India. Singapore. Malaysia.

Contents

Preface

Ishopanishad or *Isa-Upanishad* or *Isavasya Upanishad* is the 40th and the last chapter of the *Yajurved*, which is one of the four Vedas, the sacred scriptures of Hinduism. Yajurveda is a compilation of ritual-offering and worship mantras to be performed during *Havans* and *Yajnas*.

Isopanishad being the last chapter is also considered the essence of the *Yajurveda* and is also referred to as *Jnana-kand* (knowledge-chapter) of *Yajurveda*.

Isavasya Upanishad is also considered to be the first *Upanishad* and since the first *sloka* of this *Upanishad* contains the word *'Isavasyam'*, so it has been named *Isavasya Upanishad.*

'Ish or Isa' signifies *Ishwar* i.e. *Paramatma*, the Supreme or the Universal Soul and '*vasyam*' means pervaded by; thereby *'Isavasyam'* meaning that 'everything in this universe is pervaded by the *Ishwar* or the *Paramatma*'.

Apart from indicating 'what' *Paramatma* is or ought to be understood as, the teachings of this *Upanishad* have laid the foundation of *Karma-Yog* or *Karma-Marg* i.e. Path of Action and *Jnana-Yog* i.e. Path of Knowledge.

Major concepts which have been emphasized to be understood / comprehended by a devotee / seeker in *Isavasya Upanishad* include: *Paramatma* and 'His' powers; *Jnana* (knowledge), *Karma* (Action), and *Moksha* (liberation); *dheer Purusha* (steadfast and equanimous person), *Jnani* (one who has knowledge) and benefits of being a *Jnani*; *Jnana-Marg* and *Karma-Marg* and their complementarity; *Sambhuti* (One with Absolute power) and *Asambhuti* (those without absolute power) and their worship; prayer of devotee before death for *Darshan* (vision) of *Paramatma;* and finally the acceptance of physical death by a *Mumurshu* (one just before or while dying), his prayer to Paramatma and to *Agni-devta* (Fire God).

Though this *Upanishad* has only 18 slokas and is the shortest in length among all the Upanishads, yet it remains one of the most important Upanishad and is the essence of spirituality and wisdom. It is spiritually very useful for every human being in the universe, irrespective of religion, race, caste, creed and geographical location.

Raj Bhambu

March 2025

Prologue

AUM TAT SHAT AUM!!!

AUM SHANTI SHANTI SHANTI!!!

Before commenting on or attempting to explain 18 *slokas* of the *Isavasya Upanishad*, it is appropriate to have a translation of all the 18 *slokas* of this first *Upanishad,* because the original language of Vedas and Upanishads is Sanskrit. It will help the reader / seeker / devotee in first getting an overview of the whole Upanishad, before he/she starts delving deeper into each sloka of this 'essence of spirituality'.

Sloka 1

In the entire Universe, whatever animate or inanimate forms exist, they are all pervaded by *Ishwar* i.e. *Param-Atma* or the Supreme Soul. Keeping that *Param-Atma* in constant remembrance and with a feeling of dispassion and renunciation, one can enjoy this *Jagat* (universe), which is a creation of God. However, one shouldn't get attached to anyone or anything here, because who owns the impermanent and unreal wealth, pleasures and substances existing here.

Sloka 2

In this universe, one should do his *Karma* (work / action) as directed by the sacred scriptures i.e. as an offering to the *Ishwar* and aspire to live a hundred years; all the actions performed in this way (i.e. through detachment and renunciation and as an offering to *Ishwar*), a person doesn't get bound; there is no other way (for releasing oneself from the *karma-bandhan* i.e. bondage due to actions performed and resulting transmigratory cycle of rebirth).

Sloka 3

The diversified and manifold life-forms of *asuras* (demons), and hellish worlds thereof, are all pervaded by ignorant and sorrowful forms of darkness. All those human beings who kill their own *Atma* (soul), go to those hellish worlds after their death.

Sloka 4

'That' *Parameshwar* is quiescent, immutable, unstirred, firm, unalterable, unitary, absolutely still yet moving faster than thoughts in mind, the beginning of everything and omniscient; even *Indra* (King among the Gods and God of Rain) can't reach 'Him', achieve 'Him', or know 'Him', without 'His' grace and blessings. 'That' *Param-Brahman Parameshwar* can over-take the fast-moving (such as thoughts), even though being still. Drawing their powers from 'Him', *Vayu-Devta* (Wind-God) enables movement and *Indra-Dev* (God of rain) creates rain activity.

Sloka 5

'He' is movable as well as immovable; 'He' is faster than the farthest as well as closer than the closest; 'He' pervades everything in this universe; and also 'He' is outside this universe i.e. 'He' is within everything as well as beyond this universe.

Sloka 6

Such a wise one sees all the animate being of the world in *Paramatma*, and such a one also sees *Paramatma* in every living being of this universe. After this experience and being fully convinced of it, such a wise one never hates or looks down upon any living being; because he knows that irrespective of the body forms and actions thereof, every living being is pervaded by *Paramatma* and is a part of *Paramatma*, including the wise one himself. Therefore, the wise one recognizes the oneness, unity or non-duality among himself, all living beings and *Paramatma*.

Sloka 7

The *jnani* i.e. wise one, who knows *Param-Brahman Parameshwar* through personal experience, perceives every living being as a form of *Parameshwar* and pervaded by *Parameshwar* at all times. In such a unitary state, wherein the *Jnani* perceives every living being as a form of *Paramatma* i.e. one with *Paramatma*, there is no attachment or pleasure due to attachment as well as there is no pain due to worldly attachment / detachment / desires etc. Such a wise one is always in a blissful state, with no worldly or sensual feelings of pleasure or pain impacting upon his inner-self.

Sloka 8

Such a *Mahatma* (the great soul), the *Jnani*, the wise one, the one truly knowing 'Him', 'attains' *Paramatma* Himself; *Paramatma*, the effulgent, unitary, devoid of body, devoid of five basic body elements and sheaths, non-decaying, devoid of auspiciousness or inauspiciousness of *Karma*, devoid of touch through any and every medium. *Paramatma*, who is the seer of all, omniscient and the form of knowledge, all pervading, all-encompassing, self-proclaiming, eternal, and the One who has been creating all animate and inanimate parts of the universe, in accordance with *Karma* of the living beings.

Sloka 9

Those beings who worship (i.e. follow religiously and indulge in) *Avidya*, they enter the darkest realm, in the form of ignorance; while those beings who are attached to and are indulged in *Vidya* i.e. those who are delusional and proud of their knowledge, enter even more dark realms (of ignorance).

Sloka 10

By following *Vidya* i.e. *Jnana-Marg* or path of true knowledge, one gets a different result (as compared to one explained in previous sloka which one gets by following *Avidya*); by following *Karma-Marg* (path of true action) one gets a different result; thus we have heard from the *Dheer* (steadfast and wise one) beings, who have vividly explained this subject.

Sloka 11

The being, who in true sense comes to know and understand the essence and real meaning of both i.e. *Karma* (action) and *Jnana* (knowledge) together, will be able to transcend death through *Karma-Marg* actions and through *Jnana-Marg* actions, he attains the nectar of Self-realization by being one with the eternal, blissful, indestructible *Paramatma*.

Sloka 12

Those human beings who worship *Asambhuti* (i.e. *Devtas* or Gods, Saints, *Gurus*, Ancestors etc.) are destined to go into the darkest alleys of ignorance; and those who worship *Sambhuti* (i.e. *Paramatma, Parameshwar or Brahman* which is/have the absolute power) with a feeling of indulgence, obsession and delusional pride, they go to even more dark alleys of ignorance.

Sloka 13

By worshipping indestructible, eternal Brahman, one gets a different result; by worshipping perishable or non-eternal Gods-Saints/Gurus-Ancestors etc., one get different results. This is what we have heard from the *Dheer* (steadfast, equanimous wise men i.e. the Self-realized ones), who have explained this subject to us very well.

Sloka 14

Those human beings who know, understand and assimilate the true meaning of *Sambhuti* (i.e. the absolutely powerful *Paramatma*) and *Asambhuti* (i.e. those without absolute power such as devtas, saints, gurus, ancestors etc.) simultaneously, they reach beyond death through worshipping the devtas etc. and attain the supreme nectar (attain oneness with *Paramatma*) through worshipping the *Paramatma.*

Sloka 15

O *Paramatma*! Provider, nurturer and sustainer of all, the true Self! Your real Self is hidden behind the dazzling effulgence; kindly remove this veil / mantle, so that I, who devotionally worships you by following true / real path i.e. *Satvik-Marg*, can have your *Darshan* (i.e. auspicious vision of *Paramatma*).

Sloka 16

O sustainer of devotees, supreme form of knowledge, regulator (i.e. controller and restrainer) of all; the ultimate goal of all the wise seekers, divine goal of *Prajapati* (God Brahma); (I pray to you to) kindly either remove the dazzling rays of Your effulgence or remove the effulgent aura of Your divinity, (so that) I can see (i.e. experience) your divine form. With Your kind Grace, through meditation I am able to visualize 'That' (soul of the Sun), the Supreme Soul (which is your form) and I am also 'That'.

Sloka 17

Now let the *Prana* (life-giving air) and its related senses enter / merge with the immortal and total air element; let this physical body end itself in the fire element; O *Sacchidanand* (Existence-Consciousness-Bliss i.e. *Paramatma*), Lord of sacrifice, (I pray to you to) kindly remember me, kindly remember all the actions performed by me.

Sloka 18

O *Agni-devta* (i.e. the Presiding deity of the fire-element)! (I pray to you to) please carry me to the supremely blissful, serene and peaceful abode of the Paramatma, kindly take me through the auspicious path; O God! You know all my *Karmas* (deeds), therefore, all those sinful Karmas of mine which can be a hindrance, I pray to you to kindly remove them. I pray you, I pray you again and again.

AUM TAT SAT AUM

AUM SHANTI SHANTI SHANTI!!!

1. Jnana and Karma

Karma principle i.e. cause and effect principle is a well-tested, standardised and extensively explained principle for the worldly life cycle. It has been variously described by various interpreters of the sacred texts.

Broadly, this principle states that all actions and intentions behind actions of an individual *Jiva* (human being) have consequences or fruits, which will get evened-out in future, through situations or events in this or future births of that Jivatma.

Every *Karma* results in formation of *Samskara* (imprints of actions) and the same needs to be exhausted before one is able to find release from the transmigratory cycle of rebirths. This release i.e. liberation is generally referred to as *Moksha*.

The first two slokas of *Isavasya Upanishad* provide guidance to human beings as to how one (i.e. a human being, a seeker or a devotee) can liberate (i.e. attain *Moksha*) oneself from the eternal bondage of this repetitive transmigratory cycle of birth and death.

Swami Sivanand had commented that the first sloka of the *Isavasya Upanishad* lays down the rule for 'Jnana' (i.e. Knowledge), while the second sloka lays down the rule for 'Karma' (i.e. action meaning how one must act in this world). So, if the first sloka is the basis of *Jnana-Yog Siddhant*, then the second sloka is the basis for *Karma-Yog Siddhant*.

Sloka 1

In the entire Universe, whatever animate or inanimate forms exist, they are all pervaded by Ishwar i.e. Param-Atma. Keeping that Param-Atma in constant remembrance and with a feeling of dispassion and renunciation, one can enjoy this Jagat (universe) i.e. creation of God. However, one shouldn't get attached to anyone or anything here, because who owns the impermanent and unreal wealth, pleasures and substances existing here.

This 1st sloka of Isavasya Upanishad has three parts to it i.e.

- everything is pervaded by Ishwar (*sarv-vyapkata of Ishwar*);
- this universe which is a creation of Ishwar can be enjoyed by Jiva but with conditions being constant remembrance of Ishwar and dispassion and renunciation;

- Why and how of dispassion and renunciation.

Let us discuss each part in detail:

1. Everything is pervaded by Ishwar.

The Vedic scriptures emphasize that God isn't someone who sits in the seventh heaven and rules or runs the world from there but 'He' exist in every part of us, and of this universe.

Various scriptures use varied terms to describe Ishwar such as Paramatma, Brahman, Sacchidanand, Universal Soul, Supreme Soul, God etc. but here we shall use *Ishwar* or *Paramatma* to refer to the Almighty, Supreme, Omnipotent, Omnipresent, Omniscient, eternal, all blissful, effulgent, beyond the world, indescribable 'One'. This 1st Sloka of the Isavasya Upanishad highlight that the entire universe, (i.e. every minutest or the largest and animate or inanimate part of it), is pervaded by (*Sarv-Vyapt*) the *Ishwar* at all times.

It has been said by Shri Krishna in Srimadbhagvad Gita (9.4) thus:

This entire cosmic manifestation is pervaded by Me in My unmanifest form. All living beings dwell in Me and I dwell in them.

Apart from universal existence, this sloka of Gita has also highlighted that Ishwar pervades everything in 'His' unmanifest form, we aren't able to experience 'Him' through our limited sensory capabilities.

Sarv-vyapkta (universal existence) of *Paramatma* has been emphasized in *Shwetashvatar Upanishad* (6.11) thus:

There is one God; He is seated in everyone's heart; He is also everywhere in the world.

Purush Suktam, a hymn in the *Rig-Veda*, dedicated to *Purusha* i.e. the "Cosmic Being" or *Ishwar*, gives a description of the spiritual unity of the universe. It presents *Purusha* or the 'cosmic being' as both immanent in the manifested world and yet transcendent to it i.e. beyond the universe. This Suktam says:

God pervades everything that has existed and all that will exist.

It is an established scientific principle that a subtle substance will pervade a grosser substance. So, whatever is the most subtle will always pervade everything that is grosser than that. *Paramatma* being the subtlest will certainly pervade everything in this universe, which is certainly grosser than the most subtle, more minute and smaller than the smallest i.e. Ishwar.

2. Enjoyment of Jagat but with dispassion and renunciation.

Now, since this universe is a creation or sport of the supremely pure and blissful Paramatma, can or should, we humans, enjoy 'His' creation i.e. animate and inanimate wealth, pleasures and substances? And if yes, how?

To answer this, the 1st Sloka has emphasized that we can enjoy the creation, but we must keep the below in mind:

We must always keep remembering *Ishwar* while enjoying His creation i.e. Be Grateful and enjoy everything as 'His' creation.

If we do that, can or should we have the sinful feelings if we are enjoying Ishwar's creations? Should we overindulge in enjoyment? Not at all.

In Bhagvad Gita (2.64), Shri Krishna has reiterated the same aspect of detachment thus:

But who controls the mind, and is free from attachment and aversion, even while using the objects of the senses, attains the Grace of God.

In Bhagavatam (4.30.19), Lord Vishnu instructed thus:

The prefect karma-yogis, even while fulfilling their household duties, perform all their works as Yagna to me, knowing me to be the Enjoyer of all activities. They spend whatever free time they have in hearing and chanting my glories. Such people, though living in the world, never get bound by their actions.

Thus, one must keep remembering Paramatma and also the fact that everything belongs only to the Paramatma. One should live one's life with an aim to please "Him" at all times, utilizing every creation of 'His', performing every action with a devotional feeling of making an offering to 'Him' only. Further, Shri Krishna has emphasized this in Bhagvad Gita (18.46) thus:

By performing one's natural occupation, one worships the Creator from whom all living entities have come into being, and by whom the whole universe is pervaded. By such performance of work, a person easily attains perfection.

So, one can enjoy (carry-out scripture prescribed actions) this jagat (universe) remembering Ishwar constantly and without attachment (to pleasurable) and aversion (towards painful). This has also been echoed by Shri Krishna in Srimadbhagvad Gita (8.7) thus:

Therefore, always remember Me and do your duty of fighting the war. With mind and intellect surrendered to Me, you will definitely attain Me; of this, there is no doubt.

Here Shri Krishna advises Arjun to do his assigned Karma i.e. fighting the war; but even in such an intense earthly Karma of fighting a war, Arjun is being advised to remember Paramatma. This is a universal message for every human being, irrespective of profession, location and time.

3. Why and how of detachment and renunciation

It is not possible for a human being in this worldly context to develop detachment, dispassion and renunciation towards the worldly aspects.

However, once it is very clearly known and understood that this universe is temporary and unreal, it becomes easier. If we analyse scientifically and logically, it is very simple to understand that whatever gets created will ultimately get destroyed too. We can see for ourselves that in this universe, everything is temporary and perishable / destructible, including our own physical existence.

This has been highlighted by Shri Krishna in Srimadbhagvad Gita (2.14) thus:

The contact between the senses and the sense objects gives rise to momentary, fleeting perceptions of pleasure and pain or happiness and distress. These are non-permanent and temporary, and come and go like the seasons. One must learn to tolerate them without being disturbed.

In Ribhu Gita, sage Ribhu advises his disciple Nidagha thus:

There is nothing in this world whatsoever as 'anything and everything' is illusory, being based on the non-existent thoughts and therefore non-existent mind. There is nothing whatsoever of knowledge, variety of knowledge, to be known or the knower. Be of the certitude that: 'All is Brahman alone'.

If one keeps the above in mind, then he will slowly develop dispassion and renunciation towards the worldly pleasures and wealth. This is also emphasized in this Sloka i.e. one can enjoy the unreal, temporary worldly pleasures but with a feeling of dispassion and renunciation. How to do that?

One shouldn't get attached or be egoistic with feelings of I, me, mine etc. in this temporary, perishable and unreal existence. Attachment always leads to sorrow/pain for every living being, so one needs to shun the feeling of attachment to any animate or inanimate creation of *Ishwar*.

Similar to this sloka, Shri Krishna too has said in the Bhagvad Gita (3.9) thus:

Work must be done as a Yajna (pronounced as yagya) to the Supreme Lord; otherwise, work causes bondage in this material world. O son of Kunti, for the satisfaction of God, perform your prescribed duties, without being attached to the results.

In this Sloka or everywhere else in sacred scriptures as well as by saints and gurus, it has been repeatedly advised and emphasized that human beings must give-up attachment and desires in this world.

However, it needs to be remembered that this knowledge and call for detachment, dispassion and renunciation, always pertains to material attachment and desires i.e. worldly attachment and desires related to body, mind and intellect.

Spiritual attachment and desire i.e. attachment to Ishwar and desire to attain unity with 'Him' are not to be given-up; in fact they need to be cultivated and increased as they lead to purification of mind.

Thus, as told by Swami Sivanand, this sloka of Isavasya Upanishad lays down the foundation of Jnana-Yog or Jnana-Marg (i.e. Path of knowledge) by letting the devotee / seeker know and understand 'That' (Paramatma). It is 'That' about which and about whom, human beings need to know, learn, and understand in their lives.

Sloka 2

In this universe, one should do his Karma as directed by the sacred scriptures i.e. as an offering to the Ishwar and aspire to live a hundred years; all the actions performed in this way (i.e. through detachment and renunciation and as an offering to Ishwar), a person doesn't get bound; there is no other way (for releasing oneself from the karma-bandhan and resulting transmigratory cycle of rebirth).

This 2nd sloka of Isavasya Upanishad, it has been explained as to how a person needs to perform one's actions in this world.

Here, it has been emphasized that one should not harbor feelings of doership, but must offer every act of oneself as a devotional offering to the Almighty. One needs to constantly remember and contemplate that whatever one does, is not for oneself or for satisfying personal desires or for satisfying ego; but it is a devotional offering to the Almighty Paramatma.

This feeling of dedicating every act as an offering to Paramatma also stops a person from doing wrong/sinful deeds, because no one in his proper senses will wish to make a bad offering to the Paramatma.

Similar to this sloka, the same sentiment of detachment and renunciation towards all actions and dedicating one's actions to Paramatma has been highlighted by Shri Krishna in Srimadbhagvad Gita extensively.

In Bhagvad Gita (2.50-51), Shri Krishna has said:

One who prudently practices the science of work without attachment can get rid of both good and bad reactions i.e. results in this life itself. Therefore strive for Yog, which is the art of working skilfully and in proper consciousness.

The wise, endowed with equanimity of intellect, abandon attachment to the fruits of actions, which bind one to the cycle of life and death. By working in a consciousness, the wise attain the state beyond all suffering.

Further, Bhagvad Gita (5.10) has emphasized it even further, thus:

Those who dedicate their actions to God, abandoning all attachment, remain untouched by sin, just as a lotus leaf is untouched by water.

So, similar to the 2nd sloka of Isavasya Upanishad, the above 3 slokas of Bhagvad Gita have reiterated that:

A person must perform every act in way that he doesn't get bonded by act's imminent reaction (as per Karma Principle) in this life or next lives. Detachment from action as well as result thereof, renunciation and dedicating every act as an offering to the God are the surest ways to live one's life happily in this world and also not getting any bondage from the same.

It has been made easy to understand by giving example of a lotus leaf.

Though a lotus leaf owes its birth, growth and sustenance to the water, yet the leaf doesn't permit itself to be wetted. Water poured on the lotus leaf runs-off the side and don't wet the leaf itself. Similarly, a person with detachment and renunciation, though living and performing every worldly action as per Sastras, remains free from bondage if he performs all his worldly actions with complete detachment and renunciation and as an offering to the Paramatma.

This 2nd Sloka of Isavasya Upanishad has very clearly said that "there is no other way" than this, to be free from this transmigratory cycle of rebirth. It is so, because till one doesn't stop one's Karma-cycle, the resulting transmigratory cycle of birth and death to reap good/bad results of those Karmas can't stop for an individual.

Here, one must be consciously aware that when one thinks about 'Karma' i.e. action, then it is not referring to the physical action alone but to every action performed at body, mind and intellect level i.e. physical actions as well as one's thoughts, motives and intentions are included in Karma.

For example, if a person does service to the poor with an intention of gaining their respect or some social/political benefits, then that Karma binds that person and will certainly have a result at a later stage in this life or next lives.

However, if a person is invited to do a social service, he does that social service dedicating the same to Paramatma, with no ego attached i.e. I did such and such social service; and in that case there is no bondage for such a person for that action.

To conclude, teachings of these two very important slokas can be summarized as below:

- Everything in this universe, i.e. animate and inanimate, is pervaded by Ishwar, as everything has emanated from 'Him' only.
- One can enjoy His creation but only with a feeling of dispassion and detachment and keeping Ishwar in one's thoughts at all times.
- One must remember that everything in this universe is temporary, unreal, and destructible and oneself being the same as the rest of the universe, no-one owns anything in this universe. That being so, there is no need for any attachment or egoistic tendencies.
- One keeps returning to this earthly life till one doesn't stop Karma-cycle.
- To stop Karma-cycle, one has to stop performing Karma.
- However, being in this universe a person needs to perform certain actions on a daily basis, so·how can one stop Karma-cycle.
- Only those actions which are done with attachment to action (including intention, desires, motives etc.) or results thereof create bondage.

- Those actions which are done as a dedication to Ishwar and with no attachment to action (including intention, desires, motives etc.) and results thereof don't create bondage because such actions are God's actions.
- One must always indulge in actions with a Satvik intention of dedicating every thought, action, intention, and desire to Paramatma in order to free oneself from the transmigratory cycle of rebirth.

AUM TAT SAT AUM

*****

2. Asuras

After explaining the sure path to *Moksha* i.e. liberation from the transmigratory cycle of rebirth, the next sloka i.e. 3rd Sloka looks at the plight of those who follow a path that is opposite to the one given in first two slokas.

This sloka brings-in the word *Atma* (soul), so before explaining this sloka, it is worthwhile to understand the Vedic scriptural concept of *Atma* and *Param-Atma or Paramatma* (Universal or the Supreme Soul).

As highlighted in the first line of the first Sloka of Isavasya Upanishad, Paramatma pervades everything, owing to the fact that the entire universe has emanated from the "cosmic being" i.e. Paramatma (Universal or Supreme Soul). Every animate being in this universe has Atma (soul) i.e. consciousness and the physical body, mind and intellect depending on its evolution. Human beings are considered the highest evolved souls and also highest evolved in terms of body, mind and intellect.

Since every *Atma* (soul) is has emanated from or created out of the *Paramatma*, every soul is eternal and indestructible (similar to the Supreme Soul), but since every soul isn't as perfect or complete as the Supreme Soul, they aspire to reach perfection and therefore keep evolving till they reach perfection.

Once a soul reaches a level of complete perfection (similar to the perfect Paramatma), it is same as the Supreme Soul and therefore merges with the Supreme Soul i.e. attain union with Paramatma. These aspects of creation have been explained in detail in Vedas, which came first, so before Upanishads.

Another very important concept to understand is – knowledge and ignorance are often compared to light and darkness in sacred scriptures.

It is so because just as Paramatma is supremely effulgent and dazzling with light owing to its omnipotence, power and energy; knowledge too is akin to seeing light at the end of darkness.

Moreover, only knowledge of and about Paramatma is knowledge because only Paramatma is eternal and imperishable and therefore 'His' knowledge is also eternal and imperishable; rest everything is ignorance. It is so because other than Paramatma, everything else is unreal, temporary and destructible and knowledge about unreal, temporary and destructible is also of the same nature, so it is as good as ignorance only.

Sloka 3

The diversified and manifold life-forms of asuras (demons), and hellish worlds thereof, are all pervaded by ignorant and sorrowful forms of darkness. All those human beings who kill their own Atma (soul), go to those hellish worlds after their death.

The human body is the best among all types of animate bodies and is extremely rare to obtain. One gets it as a blessing from *Parameshwar* in order to liberate oneself from the transmigratory and repetitive cycle of birth and death.

Why it is a blessing? It is so because a human being is endowed with physical, mental and intellectual abilities to comprehend the real nature of *Parameshwar*, and dedicate every thought / action of his to *Parameshwar* by giving-up the sense of doership.

To waste this rare opportunity in fulfilling bodily desires, lustful cravings and ego-satisfying activities is akin to denying nectar and instead drinking filthy water.

This 3rd sloka of Isavasya Upanishad has indicated that those who waste their human life in satisfying bodily/worldly desires are the real murders of their *Atma* (soul).

We are aware that *Atma* is eternal and indestructible, so it can't be killed. However, here it is a suggestive language wherein it has been suggested that by such degrading actions (such as wasting life in satisfying bodily/worldly desires), these people are further prolonging their transmigratory life cycle.

It is so because for every additional Karma that such people indulge in, they are liable to reap the results of their Karma, thereby increasing the length of their transmigratory cycle of birth and death.

Also such people have been termed as *asuras* (demons) owing to their worldly desires, physical cravings and egotistic propensities, which result from ignorance only. By indulging more and more into such *Karmas*, these *asuras* fall even lower into the abyss of ignorance, which results in even greater sorrows.

The purport or essence of this sloka has been profoundly explained in Srimadbhagvad Gita (1.13-16), Shri Krishna has said thus:

A person with demoniac propensities thinks – 'So much wealth I have today and I will gain more according to my schemes. So much is mine now and it will increase more and more. He is my enemy and I have killed 'Him' and my other enemies will also be killed.

I am the lord of everything, the enjoyer, perfect, powerful and happy. I am the richest man and there is none as powerful and happy as I am. I shall perform sacrifices, I shall give some in charity and thus I shall rejoice.' In this way, such persons are deluded by ignorance.

Thus perplexed by various anxieties and bound by a network of illusions, they become too strongly attached to sense enjoyment and fall down into hell.

Further in Bhagvad Gita (16.19-20), Shri Krishna has said that such persons with demonic propensities may have any amount of worldly knowledge, wealth, power or designation, but they are sure to take rebirth in lower yonis (lower forms of life compared to human beings) to reap the results of their Karmas.

In addition, in Bhagvad Gita (6.5), Shri Krishna has advised that a human being must utilize his/her life for spiritual upliftment and getting free from the bondage of transmigratory cycle of rebirth and not waste it for degeneration / downfall.

Now, what is it that needs to be controlled or taken care of, so that demonic tendencies don't arise? This has been clarified in Amritbindu Upanishad, which emphasizes thus:

'It is indeed the mind that is the cause of man's bondage and liberation. The mind that is attached to sense-objects leads to bondage, while detached from sense-objects, it tends to lead to liberation.'

What is mind? It is some total of our thoughts. So, one needs to have a total control over one's thoughts but is that possible? No.

However, one can certainly direct them towards remembering Paramatma at all times, dedicating every thought, word, action, intention, motivation to 'Him' alone and thus one can get detached from this world and bring an end to one's Karma-cycle, thereby liberating oneself from the transmigratory cycle of rebirth.

AUM TAT SAT AUM

*****

3. Paramatma

Since we are to dedicate all our thoughts, desires, motives, intentions and action to Ishwar or Paramatma, then knowing, understanding and assimilating *Paramatma* is of paramount importance to the Jivatma i.e. a human being.

In that case, the next logical step for a devotee or seeker is: to know what/how of the *Paramatma*, the *Parameshwar*, which pervades everything in the entire universe and beyond.

The next two sloka, i.e. sloka 4 and 5 have tried to explain 'Him' i.e. *Ishwar* or *Paramatma*. Also, these two slokas have discussed about the *Shakti* (power) of *Paramatma*.

Why we say – tried to? Because, as explained earlier, *Paramatma* is beyond the limited comprehension ability of body, mind and intellect of a human being and also because *Paramatma* can only be experienced (*anubhav*) and not expressed about in words. In spite of that numerous scriptures and wise sages have tried to explain their *anubhav* (experience of God-realization) for guiding others to seek 'Him'.

Sloka 4

'That' Parameshwar is quiescent, immutable, unstirred, firm, unalterable, unitary, absolutely still yet moving faster than thoughts in mind, the beginning of everything and omniscient; even Indra (King among the Gods and God of Rain) can't reach 'Him', achieve 'Him', or know 'Him', without 'His' grace and blessings. 'That' Param-Brahman Parameshwar can over-take the fast-moving (such as thoughts), even though being still. Drawing their powers from 'Him', Vayu (Wind-God) enables movement and Indra-Dev (God of rain) creates rain activity.

This sloka has tried to explain that the all-pervading *Parameshwar* is all-powerful, omnipotent, omniscient, omnipresent, and unalterable, and the power behind everything, be it air, light, rain, animate or inanimate universe.

Also, this sloka highlights the fact that He is 'the beginning of everything' i.e. the 'Cosmic Being' from whom everything else has emanated. He is omniscient and therefore knows everything but even the Kings of Gods, Indra cannot know Him. In that case, He is certainly beyond the comprehension of limited capabilities of human mind and intellect. That is why it is said that He can only be experienced but can't be reached, achieved or known, without His grace and blessings.

In Yoga-Vasishtha, Muni Vasishtha ji has also explained the *swarup* (form) of Paramatma thus:

The pure, conscious Paramatma is neither a topic of vision nor of disclosure; neither He is close nor far-off, but He can only be experienced; and He is ever established with equanimity. The pure Sacchidanand (Existence-Consciousness-Bliss) Paramatma is without any body-form, senses, mind-form, desires, knowledge or worldly-form, as we know them; but He is beyond all these, surpassing everything and the Supreme and transcendent.

He is neither real nor unreal, neither with form nor without form, and is beyond time, space and objectification. He is only Brahman and consciousness. Everything in this world is pervaded by that supreme and pure consciousness, but He Himself is not pervaded by anything. Whatever animate or inanimate forms are visible or not visible in this universe and beyond are pervaded by That Supreme, Effulgent Consciousness, which is named by us humans as Paramatma, Brahman or Parameshwar.

He is firm and unitary yet travels faster than thoughts; He is already present where mind reaches (implying that He travels faster than thoughts); mind or thoughts can't even reach where He is already present (meaning He is beyond thoughts and mind of us human beings). He is the most ancient and of the form of knowledge; He knows everyone or everything but none can know Him fully, not even Gods or Rishis. He can only be experienced.

On similar lines, in Srimadbhagvad Gita (10.2), Shri Krishna has also explained the all-knowing, all-powerful Parameshwar (i.e. Himself) thus:

Neither celestial Gods nor the great sages know of my origin. I am the source from which the Gods and great seers come.

The next sloka i.e. sloka 5 has further explained the unthinkable powers and pervasiveness / expanse of Paramatma.

Sloka 5

'He' is movable as well as immovable; 'He' is faster than the farthest as well as closer than the closest; 'He' pervades everything in this universe; and also 'He' is outside this universe i.e. 'He' is within everything as well as beyond this universe.

For us humans, whatever seems contradictory and unthinkable, from the point-of-view of feelings, logic, quality and action, is very much a reality of *Parameshwar* and that is his unthinkable power.

In Srimadbhagvad Gita (7.7), Paramatma is described as *the Supreme or ultimate basis / stratum as well as cause of the universe; and that is why He pervades everything, is inside as well as outside everything, including this Jagat (universe).*

Shri Krishna states about His Supreme position in this universe by emphasizing that *He is the*

Substratum over which this entire creation (not only this universe) exists; He is the Creator, Sustainer, and Annihilator. Similar to beads strung in a thread, which can move in their place, ParamAtma has given individual Jiva-Atma the free will to act as they wish, yet their existence is bound to Him.

In *Brahm-Samhita* (5.1), Lord *Brahma* referring to Shri Krishna (indicating Krishna to be *Parameshwar*) prays thus:

Shri Krishna (Parameshwar) is the Supreme Lord, omniscient, and infinite bliss. He is without beginning and end, the origin of all, and the cause of all.

In Srimadbhagvad Gita (13:14) Shri Krishna states that *God's senses are everywhere* and then in the very next sloka (13.15) He states thus:

Though He perceives all sense-objects, yet He is devoid of senses. He is unattached to everything, and yet He is sustainer of all. Although He is without attributes, yet He is enjoyer of the three modes of material nature.

These seemingly contradictory powers of *Paramatma* have been stated in *Brahma-Vivarta Purana* thus: "*The Supreme Lord is the reservoir of innumerable contradictory attributes*".

These seemingly contradictory attributes seem contradictory only to human beings because of their limited capabilities of body, mind and intellect and their inability to comprehend *Paramatma*. A human mind, with its limited intellect wants to conceptualize *Paramatma* in a form (space aspect) and that is not possible because unlike humans who are limited in space and time, Paramatma isn't.

In Ribhu Gita (6th Chapter of Sri Shiva Rahasyam), *Paramatma* is referred to as *Brahman* and in its chapter titled 'Brahman is All' (*Sarvam Brahman*), *Brahman (i.e. Paramatma)* has been described in detail by sage Ribhu thus:

- All is indeed Brahman alone. Brahman alone is the great mystic design, the fruit of action, the great aphorisms, the whole world, the sentient and the insentient, the attributes and qualities, 'I' and the transcendental light, the supreme Brahman.

- Brahman alone is the limitless Self, the transcendental bliss, the supreme knowledge, the object, the beings and whatever little there is, is Brahman alone. Brahman alone is the ultimate shore, the triad of states, the multiplicity, the supreme transcendence, the body, the form and the formless, senses of sound, smell, touch, the mind and the essence.

- The secretive, the external, the eternal are all Brahman alone. In 'That Thou Art', the words 'That', 'Thou' i.e. you and 'Art' are all Brahman only. The beginning and end of the world and the state of the beginning and end of the world as well as the beings and non-beings are all Brahman alone. I am only Brahman – there is no doubt of this. Whatever in the least there is – is Brahman only.

- Truth and existence, waking, dreaming, deep sleep and turiya (fourth state) are Brahman only. I am the supreme Brahman only. Being, regard for the Guru, the noble attitude of the disciple and liberation are indeed Brahman alone. The before and the beyond, the complete and the eternal, the manifested are all Brahman only. Being-Consciousness-Bliss is Brahman. Brahman alone is perfect, complete and eternal.

- The joyous Brahman is manifesting everywhere as the adorable form. The individual exhibiting Satvik (pure and auspicious) tendencies shines as Shiva always. The individual with sinful traits remains to experience hell. Brahman alone shines as the senses, the objects and the behaviors and activities. All joy and all knowledge personified is Brahman alone. The operation of Maya (illusion) is said to be Brahman alone.

- The process of sacrifice, the heart-space, the essence of liberation, the pure and the impure, the cause of all and the affairs of the earth are Brahman alone. All is indeed Brahman alone. All the days, the silent Self of the beings, the ever satisfied Self and the essential import of the Vedas is Brahman alone. It is Brahman alone that is realized through meditation and the accomplishment of all the yogas is also said to be Brahman only.

- Brahman appears as the diverse forms because of the limiting adjuncts i.e. capabilities of senses, mind and intellect. When all this is realized only as an illusion, nothing exists by its own virtue. Brahman alone shines as the world, as the people, as the form, assembly of sages and forms of meditation. Brahman alone is forms of Divine, as absolute and relative knowledge, pure and enlightened Self, the Paramesvara.

- Brahman alone is the highest bliss, the expanding light of consciousness, the highest knowledge. Brahman alone is the Self of the living beings, the form of sacrifice, the sacred offering. All is indeed Brahman alone. Brahman alone is the whole world, the Guru and disciple, all the accomplishments, all the mantras, japa and all the actions. Brahman alone is all peacefulness, the core of heart, all unitariness, the state of imperishable and the attribute of imperishable. Brahman alone is of the form of Brahman. All is indeed Brahman alone.

- Brahman alone is the abode of truth and without doubt, Brahman alone am I. Brahman alone is import of the word 'I' and of the word 'That' and of the word 'you'. Brahman alone is Paramesvara. All is indeed Brahman alone. Whatever supreme there is, is Brahman alone, the great devotion and objective knowledge. Without doubt, Brahman is all - this entire world, you and whatever there is. All is indeed Brahman.

- Brahman alone is only Brahman, the Self, by itself, is only Bliss and is all so attainable. Brahman alone is all, only Brahman and anything apart from Brahman is ever unreal. Brahman alone is the import of all sacred utterances, the supreme state, truth and untruth, devoid of beginning and end, the one eternal joy, bliss of consciousness. Brahman alone is the One, without any doubt.

- Brahman alone is Consciousness itself, self-abiding, rid of adjuncts, the eternal all, all that is pure, ever easily accomplished, the truth of truths. Brahman alone is happiness, verily happiness, the blissful Self, the ever spoken of. All is indeed Brahman alone. Brahman alone is the complete Brahman, the one witness of all, the lavish abode, the all-round perfect Self, the undiminishing essence, the devotion, the Self of all beings, the embodiment of happiness and the eternally satisfied Self.

- Brahman alone is the Self that is non-dual only, the ethereal space-like Isvara, the joy of heart. There is nothing higher than Brahman and apart from Brahman, there is no world either. Apart from Brahman I am not I, you are not you, is no joy, no fruit, not a blade of grass. Any state apart from Brahman is a myth.

- The world apart from Brahman is an illusion. There is nothing apart from Brahman. All is indeed Brahman alone. Any action, body, mind, intellect, egoity, this world apart from Brahman is a myth and an illusion. All is indeed Brahman alone.

Further, Chhandogya Upanishad (3.14.1) has highlighted the universality and omnipresence of Paramatma while stating: *"sarvam khalvidam Brahman" i.e. everywhere is Brahman.*

Thus, these two slokas i.e. 4-5 of Isavasya Upanishad (and several other scriptures) have tried to explain *Paramatma / Parameshwar / Brahman* and His powers (i.e. *Shakti*), who is beyond the beyond and who is even beyond the imaginative powers of Gods and Rishis.

AUM TAT SAT AUM

*****

4. Jnani

The next two slokas, i.e. 6 and 7, describe the *Jnani* (wise) human beings who know 'Him' i.e. Paramatma through experience. Knowing Him only through reading or listening about Him is similar to estimating depth of water looking at its surface and without even getting down in water.

None can know 'Him' or describe Him, because He can only be experienced and even those experiences about Him, can't be fully explained through written or spoken words. It is so because He is beyond human senses and capabilities. Even those, who have had experience about 'Him' or of 'Him', are similar to someone who got a glimpse of Himalayas and saw one peak of Himalayas and then saying that he has seen or experienced the beauty and vastness of Himalayas.

Sloka 6

Such a wise one sees all the animate being of the world in Paramatma, and such a one also sees Paramatma in every living being of this universe. After this experience and being fully convinced of it, such a wise one never hates or looks down upon any living being; because he knows that irrespective of the body forms and actions thereof, every living being is pervaded by Paramatma and is a part of Paramatma, including the wise one himself. Therefore, the wise one recognizes the oneness, unity or non-duality among himself, all living beings and Paramatma.

Once someone starts believing that entire universe, including himself, is part of Paramatma then there is no hate or jealousy or anger towards anything or anyone and such a wise one develops equanimity and steadfastness in his behavior.

In Srimadbhagvad Gita (6:29) such a wise one has been described thus:

The true yogis, uniting their consciousness with God, see with equal eye, all living beings in God and God in all living beings.

When a *Jnani* has experienced *Paramatma*, such a wise one becomes one with 'Him' and knows that just as the same gold is present in all the ornaments made of gold, Paramatma is present in all living beings.

Narada Panchtantra (22) has explained the same thus:

Just as the sun, while remaining in one place, spreads light everywhere, similarly the Parameshwar, by His various energies pervades and sustains everything that exists.

The wise ones, in the light of Paramatmic knowledge, sees everything in connection with and in common with Paramatma.

In Yoga-Vasishtha, a *tatva-gyani* (i.e. the wise one knowing the essence of *Paramatma* and the knower of divine truth), has been described as one who, having known 'That' should be known, lives every moment with steadfast devotion to 'Him'. Because of this state of his mind, the Jnani is relieved of his past Karmas and he has no attachment or detachment towards his present actions, thereby he stops his *Karma* cycle. *Moksha* or liberation from transmigratory cycle of rebirth for such a wise one stops in this lifetime itself.

Muni Vasishtha further described such a wise one thus:

Such a one is ever supremely peaceful, with his mind not affected by worldly activities and he engages in every activity in such a way that he dedicates all his thoughts and actions to Paramatma. Further, such a wise one is ever desire-less, steadfast and devoted to 'Him' at all times, is ever without any egoistic tendency, has no feelings of pleasure or pain, sees 'His' presence in every living being and is ever established in a supremely conscious, non-dual state i.e. a state similar to that of Paramatma or Brahman.

In the same *Sarg* (canto) of Yoga-Vasishtha, Muni Vasishtha has also described characteristics of an ignorant one i.e. one who doesn't know

Paramatma because such a one hasn't experienced the bliss of Parameshwar as yet.

The ignorant one has been described as one whose mind is full of worldly desires, who is oblivious of Paramatma, who is always after worldly pleasures and is ever trying to avoid pains inflicted on him by attachment, non-achievement of desired results of his actions etc.

Such an ignorant one is similar to an animal tied to a tree-truck by a rope, which prevents his escape i.e. similar to the animal he is also tied to his worldly transmigratory cycle (tree-truck) through his mind (rope).

Sloka 7

The wise one, who knows Param-Brahman Parameshwar through personal experience, perceives every living being as a form of Parameshwar and pervaded by Parameshwar at all times. In such a unitary state, wherein the Jnani perceives every living being as a form of Paramatma i.e. one with Paramatma, there is no attachment or pleasure due to attachment as well as there is no pain due to worldly attachment/detachment/desires etc. Such a wise one is always in a blissful state, with no worldly or sensual feelings of pleasure or pain impacting upon his inner-self.

Shri Krishna, in Srimadbhagvad Gita (5.18) emphasized the same thus:

The truly learned one, with the eyes of divine knowledge and humbleness (arising out of divine knowledge), sees with equal vision a Brahmin, a cow, an elephant, and a dog-eater.

A Brahmin (who doesn't eat any meat product), a cow, an elephant and a dog-eater (dog-eater is considered an outcaste) are all equal for the one with divine knowledge.

Also this sloka of Srimadbhagvad Gita has highlighted the fact that knowledge of Paramatma brings humbleness for the wise one and he doesn't take pride in his knowledge or look-down upon those who don't have 'His' knowledge.

Thus, once a human being has known *Paramatma* through personal experience, when he starts visualizing *Paramatma* in every living being, when his vision has turned *Paramatmik* (i.e. Paramatma-centric), then he is able to Paramatma eternally and everywhere.

In such a blessed state, such a *Jnani*, the wise one, is free from the worldly pleasures and pains. He is ever in such a blissful state that the feelings of sensual/worldly pleasures/pain don't even enter his mind. Though he is seemingly engaged in worldly activities and others also see him as such, yet he is only an instrument of God-play and these worldly activities don't pierce his inner tranquility and peace.

In Yoga-Vasishtha, Muni Vasishtha Ji has explained this state of a self-realized one through various stories and characters therein and as to how those exalted souls reached such a blissful state of oneness (*Ekatva*) with Paramatma. King Sikhidhwaj, his wife Chudala, Lord Brahaspati's son Kach etc. had known *Paramatma* through personal experience.

Lord Brahma's son sage Ribhu had reached this state after receiving Atma-Jnana (Self-Knowledge) from Bhagwan Shiva Himself. Sage Ribhu, in the Ribhu Gita, has explained the state of the one who has known the Knowable i.e. Paramatma, through personal experience, thus:

Sacchidanand (i.e. Existence-Consciousness-Bliss or Paramatma) is by itself the core of the essence of all the Vedas and the Puranas and the entire universe and beyond. This alone is the supreme Brahman, affliction-less and attainable by knowledge.

I am You and You are I; and everything, including I and You, is Brahman. (You is indicative of everything else other than oneself in this universe).

He further goes the *neti-neti* (not this – not this) path to describe the oneness of everything and everyone with Paramatma, by denying all the perceivable differences.

Sage Ribhu elaborated on the state of an *Atma-jnani* i.e. the one who has realized his real-Self by explaining how such a person views everything. For such a one:

- For an *Atma-jnani*, there is no difference, no duality or pair of opposites, no difference and nothing devoid of differences. There is nothing as 'This alone am I', nothing that is decay-less and beyond the beyond, no outside, no inside, no 'I', no will and no form.

- For an *Atma-jnani*, there is no truth, none who has renounced, no talks, no corruption of values, no quality, no qualified statement, no mental certainty, no limitation, nothing pervading and no unreal fruits.

- For an *Atma-jnani*, there is no Guru, no disciple, nothing fixed, nothing auspicious or inauspicious, nothing uniform or of differing forms, no liberation and nothing that binds.

- For an *Atma-jnani*, there is no meaning for the words '*aham*' or 'that', no senses or the objects, no doubt, no conviction, nothing of the form of peace, no non-duality, nothing above or below, no attribute, no sorrow, no pleasure or pain.

- For an *Atma-jnani*, there is no body, no sign, neither cause nor the absence of cause, no conclusion, nothing mysterious, no transcendental space, no *Karma* that is accumulated nor that is yet to be realized, no truth, no you or I, no ignorance, no knowledge, no fool, and no Pandit.

- For an *Atma-jnani*, there is no hell, no liberation and nothing purifying, no craving, no learning, no knowledge, no learner, no, deity, no death, no life, no satisfaction, nothing enjoyable, and no undivided unitary existence.

- For an *Atma-jnani*, there is no will, no world, no wakefulness or sovereignty, not even a trifle of the defect of 'equality' whatsoever, no illusion of counting the fourth state, no 'all', no impure, nothing adorable, no morality, no world, no plurality, and no admixture of other sayings.

- For an *Atma-jnani*, there is no satsang or lack of *satsang*, no *Brahman*, no inquiry, no practice, no speaker, no ablution, no holy-waters, no merit, no sin, no defect-causing actions, and nothing related to the Self, to the physical or to the divine.

- For an *Atma-jnani*, there is no birth or death anywhere, no states of waking, dream or sleep, no realms of the earth or the nether-worlds, no victory or defeat, no lowly, no fear, no sensuality, no quick death, nothing unthinkable, no one guilty, and nor the illusion of sacred lore.

- For an *Atma-jnani*, there are no *gunas i.e. sattva, rajas or tamas*, no *Saivism*, no *Vedanta*, no sacred study or the related interest, no bondage nor liberation, no identity such as male or female or transgender, and no permanent state.

- For an *Atma-jnani*, there is no praise, no slander, no hymn, no eulogy, nothing Vedic, no scriptures nor any commandments, no drinking, no emaciation, no joy, no arrogance or absence of it, no mood or lack of it, no caste, no name and no form.

- For an *Atma-jnani*, there is nothing excellent, nothing not-excellent, nothing virtuous nor anything non-virtuous, no stainlessness, no individual soul, no peace, no manifestation of peace, nothing attainable, no restraint of senses and mind, no transformation and no defect.

- For an *Atma-jnani*, there is no world of transient beings (*jiva*), no transmigratory cycle of *vasanas* (desires) and *Karma* or one full of ignorance, no world of distinctive traits, no world of the form of Vedas, no cycle of *Sastras* and *agamas*, no world as separate, and no variance causing differences.

- For an *Atma-jnani*, there is no reckoning of differences or non-differences, no imagining of defects or the absence of defects, no world of peace and peacelessness, and no transmigratory cycle of attributes or absence of attributes.

- An *Atma-jnani*, the one who has experienced 'Him' through personal experience, such a one is established with and in the thought of 'everything being Brahman' thus:

There is nothing whatsoever in the least, nothing of the 'I' anywhere, nothing of what is called 'Maya' and nothing associated with Maya, no righteousness and no persecution of Dharma. This is indeed the supreme Brahman, the affliction-less nectar of knowledge.

So, as per sage Ribhu, for such a wise one there are no differences whatsoever and everything is Paramatma, pervaded by Paramatma.

Thus, these two slokas of Isavasya Upanishad indicate the state of the Jnani (the wise ones) who have known 'Him' (i.e. *Paramatma*) through personal experience.

AUM TAT SAT AUM

*****

5. Gains for the Jnani

In the next sloka, i.e. sloka 8, it is explained as to what does the *Jnani* (i.e. the wise one), who knows *Param-Brahman Parameshwar* and sees 'Him' everywhere, gain from knowing 'Him' i.e. *Paramatma.*

Sloka 8

Such a Mahatma (the great soul), the Jnani, the wise one, the one truly knowing 'Him', 'attains' Paramatma Himself; Paramatma, the effulgent, unitary, devoid of body, devoid of five basic body elements and sheaths, non-decaying, devoid of auspiciousness or inauspiciousness of Karma, devoid of touch through any and every medium. Paramatma, who is the seer of all, omniscient and the form of knowledge, all pervading, all-encompassing, self-proclaiming, eternal, and the One who has been creating all animate and inanimate parts of the universe, in accordance with Karma of the living beings.

So effectively this sloka has indicated that 'knowing Him is attaining Him' i.e. the wise one, who is able to know *Paramatma* through experience, is not only able to able experience 'Him' but such a one also attains *Ekatva* (oneness) with the *Paramatma*, by being one with 'Him' i.e. such a Jnani realizes one's *Ekatva* (i.e. oneness or unity) with *Paramatma*. He realizes that he is *Brahman* himself.

Once a *Jnani* has realized his oneness with Paramatma, his *Karma* cycle ends, by the Grace and blessings of Paramatma and he is released from the transmigratory cycle or rebirth i.e. for such a *Jnani*, his present life on earth is the last one and there is no further rebirth. So, such a *Jivatma* (soul of the jiva) has freed itself from the clutches of birth-death cycle and attains *Moksha*.

In more recent times, several Rishi-Munis such as Raman Maharishi, Neem Karoli Baba, Trailingaswami, Shyama Charan Lahiri, Nisargdatt Maharaj, Sri Ramakrishna Paramhans, Sri Yukteshwar Giri, Swami Yoganand and scores of other Jnani sages reached the supreme stage, wherein they had realized their union with Paramatma. Such a state is described as *Jivanmukti* or *Videhmukti* in spiritual parlance.

What is the state of a *Jivanmukta* (the liberated one) or *Videhmukta* at physical/mental/intellectual levels? What does he think about himself and about the world? Does the physical life end for a

Jivanmukta or a *Videhmukta*? If not, how does he behave or carry-out his daily activities?

The state of such a *Jnani*, referred to as *Jivanmukta* and *Videhmukta* has been described in great details in the Yoga-Vasishtha as well as in Ribhu Gita.

In Ribhu Gita, Sage Ribhu has used the words *Brahman*, consciousness (*chetna or chaitnya*), and awareness, the Supreme Self etc. for *Param-Atma or Paramatma*; while sage Vasishtha has used the terms *Paramatma, Param-Brahman, Sacchidanandghan* (mass of existence-consciousness-bliss) etc. However, the essence is the same i.e. the 'Cosmic Being', the Supreme or the Universal Soul, the *Sacchidanand, Param-Atma* or *Param-Ishwar*, as has been described earlier in sloka 1 in 1st Chapter.

Jivanmukta (the liberated One)

The traits of a *Jivanmukta* according to Yoga-Vasishtha and Ribhu Gita are:

1. A *Jivanmukta* is of firm certitude and is rooted in the conviction that he is the Self or *Atma* alone and that the Self (i.e. *Atma*) is Consciousness (i.e. *Paramatma*), without doubt and that he himself is this *Brahman (Paramatma)* alone.

2. A *Jivanmukta* is of firm certitude - I am beyond the triad of body (body, mind, intellect) and

without a trace of ego, devoid of all attachments and that I am serene as the ever-blissful Self.

3. His finality is *Paramatma* only, his nature is *Paramatma* alone, and he doesn't recollect otherness but realizes the Self everywhere and is the eternal and perfect Self everywhere.

4. A *Jivanmukta* is of unitary nature, the tranquil Self, devoid of thoughts of separateness, bereft of even a trace of existence, and has no mind, no intellect, no egoity and no senses.

5. *Jivanmukta* is one who is of the final certitude – I have no defects, no body, no vital airs, no *Maya* (illusion of the world), no desires, no anger, nothing at all i.e. not even eyes, ears, nose, tongue, no distinctive traits, no mind and no gender, no bondage in this or any other world, and no waking, sleep and dream states and not even no *turiya* (fourth) state.

6. A *Jivanmukta* is always established in *Brahman* and knows, believes and behaves with the certitude that - All 'this' is not mine at all, all 'that' is none of mine either. The world whatever, wherever, whenever - I have none of it in the least, I alone am. I have no time, no space, no object, no state, no ablution, no eating, no holy waters, no services, no deity and no temple.

7. For a *Jivanmukta*, there is no bondage, no birth, no knowledge, no position, no speech, no

merit, no sin, no body and I have nothing auspicious and nothing to see. For him there is no sound, no touch, no form, no taste, no life, no everything, not the least of anything, no vitality, no being, no possessions, nothing anywhere.

8. He has nothing in liberation, no duality, no Vedas, no distance, no Guru, no disciple, no teaching, nothing anywhere that is exalted, no earth, no water, no light, no space, no duty, no Brahma, no Vishnu, no Rudra, no sun and no Karma.

9. *Jivanmukta* is one who is established thus – I have no report, no statement, no lineage, no caste, no learning, no vibration, no sound, no aim, no worldly existence and no meditation. I have no cold, no heat, no attachment, no worship, no repetition of sacred sounds or syllables, no mantra, no homa, no day and no night.

10. I have no fear, no food, no thirst, no hunger, no self, no 'before', no 'after', no above, no below, no direction and no mind. I have no past, no present, no future, no sanctification, and no purification. I have no work. The one is settled thus is a *jivanmukta*.

11. A *Jivanmukta* is always established thus: I don't have either 'Who am I?' nor 'this', nor 'another', and nor 'oneself'. I have nothing whatsoever, no certitude. I have no flesh, no blood, no marrow, no excreta, no kindness, no being.

12. I have no anxiety, no greed, nothing subsidiary, no fame and no philosophy. I have nothing at all. I have nothing white or blue or separateness. There is no abidance or 'myself' for me. Such a one who is stabilized thus is called a *jivanmukta.*

13. I have no illusion, no knowledge, nothing that is secret, no caste and not little to meditate upon. I have nothing to accept and nothing to relinquish. I have nothing to laugh about and no synchronizing and no divine. The one who is established thus is called a *jivanmukta.*

14. I have no pledge, no guilt, no grief, no pleasure and no object anywhere that is inferior. For me, there is neither knowledge nor knower, neither knowable nor myself. I have nothing at all. Such a *Jnani* (the wise one) who is resolved thus is called a *jivanmukta.*

15. For me there is no 'to you', no 'to myself', no 'outside you', no 'me'. For me there is no Guru, none at all. I have no dullness, no temple, no fatigue and no auspiciousness. Such a one who is rooted in the beatitude 'not for me, not for me' is called a *jivanmukta.*

16. I have no lineage, no aphorisms, nothing that is suitable, no grace, nothing in the least. I have no self, no oneself, no heaven, no fruit, nothing to be condemned. One who thus contemplates is called a *jivanmukta.*

17. I have no practice, no education, no peace, no restraint and no tenement. I have nothing that causes pain, no doubt, no sleep, no mind and no alternative. Such an accomplished one is called a *jivanmukta*.

18. I have no old age, no childhood, not even youth, no death and no darkness. I have no world and no enjoyment. Such a one who remembers 'I have nothing whatsoever' and who has found 'I have no silence' is called a *jivanmukta*.

This state of being a '*jivanmukta*' is the goal of the *Yogis* and the *Sadhaks* (i.e. spiritual seekers) and is difficult to be explained in words because it is generally beyond the understanding and comprehension of human mind and intellect.

Videhmukta

The other state of such a *Jnani*, the wise one who has attained his oneness with Paramatma is referred to as *Videhmukti*. As per Sage Ribhu and Sage Vasishtha, a *Videhmukta* is - one who 'does not recollect what is discarded and what is not' (i.e. one liberated or freed from the body). When the last binding chain (i.e. body) drops off and a *Jivanmukta* attains *Mahasamadhi*, then he is termed as *Videhmukta*.

Traits of a *Videhmukta* Jivatma have been described thus:

1. One who is of the form of *Brahman (Paramatma)*, the ever peaceful Self, freed from liberation and also from unitary Self, without any other form, the ever joyous, the Self of all, the Self of all beings, with an abiding form and of supreme silence, the witness alone is verily the *videhamukta*.

2. Renouncing all such convictions as 'It is all' or 'There is none', leaving all other convictions and established in the certitude 'I am Brahman and not other' and the one for whom the body is a Bliss is verily the *videhamukta*.

3. One who does not think 'I am the Self, the supreme Self, verily the Self', who does not remember the Self even in the least anywhere, anytime and one who is rooted in one's own Nature is verily the *videhamukta*.

4. Abiding in the silence, silence alone, in the certitude that all is silence and not else in the least, one who is the supreme Self, above qualities, not acceding to the notion 'The Self of all', one who is devoid of any significance, and one who is great by all parameters is a *videhamukta*.

5. For a *videhamukta*, there are no differences of time, space, object, oneself and none in the least. For such a one 'I, you, this, that, he, this one' are not felt even in the least.

6. One who is of the certitude as being devoid of qualities, the eternal Self devoid of Self, the void

Self, the universal Self devoid of universe, the Self of time, the cause of time, the Self of gods devoid of gods is a *videhamukta*.

7. One who is devoid of all concepts, who is of the nature of *Sacchidanand* (Being-Consciousness-Bliss) alone, who doesn't conclude 'I am established thus', whose conclusion is that all doesn't exist, and that there never is any enlightened, is alone the *videhamukta*.

8. One who has no settled notions regarding individual soul, *Isvara*, temple, *Vedas, Sastra*, I and has no notions such as 'such alone is Brahman' is verily a *videhamukta*.

9. *Videhamukta* is the one whose certitude is that I and the entire world are *Brahman (Paramatma)* alone and that there is not a little as separate from Paramatma. Such a one is void of the certitudes 'All this is only *Chaintnya* (consciousness), I am *Chaintnya* (consciousness) alone'.

10. *Videhamukta* is the one who is ever disposed as consciousness alone, comfortably seated within, inwardly blissful, who is of the form of unlimited Self, subtler than the subtlest, immaculate, transcending even *turiya* (the fourth state), the supreme bliss.

11. *Videhamukta* is the one who is without even name, the Self of all, the formless, not an atheist

either, whose self is the supreme Brahman, who transcends the fourth state, transcends himself and transcends even this he is all-being, is *Sam-bhav* (i.e. equanimous and steadfast) in all auspicious and inauspicious times.

12. Equipoised in bondage as well as in liberation, the Self of all, the inner Self, the Self of the universe, the supreme Self, the perfect Self everywhere, ever beyond the supreme, the limitless Self alone - is the *videhamukta.*

13. The Self that is not wisdom and is devoid of wisdom, that which is not ignorance and is devoid of ignorance, with that is neither truth nor untruth, who has no meditation, who is end of meditation, who is neither the goal nor devoid of goal, who 'Is not and who 'Is' – alone is *videhamukta.*

14. *Videhamukta* is one - For whom there is no body whatsoever, for whom there is no remembering of anything in the least, for whom the mind is non-existent, for whom consciousness alone is, all forms of mind are given-up, all modifications of qualities and their absence is terminated, for whom there is no time and space, nothing to comprehend and remember even if supreme and one who has renounced even certainty and conviction.

15. Such a One has bliss of the earthly abundance as well as of the transcendental and he is bereft of all material enjoyment. A *Videhmukta* is

one who is beyond the modes of mind, who doesn't illumine them, who is devoid of all mental activity, who has no remembrance of the body (neither gross nor subtle) at the time of physical death, so he has no fear of death too.

16. One who is the pure essence of the Vedanta, who abides in the pure and serene Self, who has cleansed that distinction too, who is enjoying the nectarine essence and elixir of Brahman / Paramatma and one who is immersed in the immortal elixir of *Brahman / Paramatma* alone is the *videhamukta*.

17. Intoxicated by the vigor of Brahmic Bliss, suffused with the essence of Brahmic nectar, one who ever reposes in the Self that is Brahman is the *videhamukta*.

Sages such as Sri Raman Maharishi, Trailingaswami ji, Sri Ramakrishna Paramhans and many more were *Videhmukta* sages, who roamed on this sacred land, and even while being a *Jivanmukta* and retaining body in this world and also after attaining *Videhmukti*, they blessed and keep blessing millions through their sheer physical or subtle presence.

In Srimadbhagvad Gita (6.9), Shri Krishna has described the state of such Yogis thus:

The yogis look upon all – well-wishers, friends, foes, the pious, and the sinners – with an impartial intellect.

The yogi who is of equal intellect towards friend, companion and foe, neutral among enemies and relatives, and unbiased between the righteous and sinful, is considered to be distinguished among humans.

Such sages or yogis sees everyone as manifestation of Paramatma. Endowed with this level of vision, Lord Hanuman says: '*siyaram sab jag jani*' (Ramayan) i.e. I see the face of Sita-ram in everyone and everywhere in this universe.

Thus, for a jnani, knowing Paramatma and attaining oneness with Paramatma, through experience, not only ends worldly, bodily, mental pains and sorrows, but by being established in Paramatma, such wise ones also ensure *Moksha* i.e. a Jnani is freed from the vicious transmigratory cycle of birth and death.

AUM TAT SAT AUM

*****

6. Vidya / Avidya

Next 3 slokas of Isavasya Upanishad, i.e. sloka 9, 10, and 11, explain the essence, the substance or the real meaning of *Vidya* (i.e. knowledge) and *Avidya* (i.e. ignorance).

In this chapter, it has been highlighted that the knowledge of and knowledge of the means of attainment of *Parameshwar* i.e. knowing 'Him' and attaining 'Him' is the real '*Vidya*' (i.e. Knowledge). At the same time, indulgence in or enjoyment of worldly pleasures and desire for attainment of heavenly abodes through worldly *Karmas* (actions) has been referred as '*Avidya*' (i.e. ignorance).

Only the one who understands the real essence of and difference between '*Jnana-Marg*' (knowledge-path) and '*Karma-Marg*' (path of action) through *Vidya*, (and subsequently follows either path earnestly or both paths complementing each other), will be able to attain results accordingly, as explained in detail in 1st Sloka of Isavasya Upanishad.

At the same time, it is not possible for one to follow the path of *Avidya* (ignorance) or indulge in *Avidya* i.e. indulge in actions directed towards attainment of worldly pleasures and then attain oneness with Paramatma.

Sloka 9

This sloka describes the misery, misfortune or predicament of those who try to follow either path, without actually knowing and understanding the real difference between *Vidya* and *Avidya* i.e. real knowledge or knowledge of 'The Real' and ignorance.

Those beings who worship (i.e. follow religiously and indulge in) Avidya, they enter the darkest realm, in the form of ignorance; while those beings who are attached to and are indulged in Vidya i.e. those who are delusional and proud of their knowledge, enter even more dark realms (of ignorance).

This sloka has explained that those beings who indulge in *Avidya* i.e. indulge in worldly actions for satisfying their sensual desires and worldly pleasures are destined to keep repeating the vicious transmigratory cycle of rebirth i.e. keep taking birth and keep suffering sorrows and pains in this world. Such beings never get liberation from the cycle of birth and death and keep experiencing miseries in this world, life after life.

On the other hand, there are those who keep reading, repeating and boasting about their bookish knowledge of *Sastras* (i.e. religious scriptures), without actually understanding and realizing the essence, purport or the real meaning of the scriptural knowledge. Such beings fall in even greater abyss of ignorance, because by doing so, they are solidifying and strengthening their egoistic tendencies and those strengthened tendencies never let them understand the true meaning and essence of sacred scriptures.

The above difference between *Vidya* and *Avidya* has been explained in the Ribhu Gita thus:

Sage Ribhu tells his disciple Nidagha that everything in this universe and beyond is Brahman alone and the supreme Brahman is to be comprehended through the Vedas and especially through 'Vidya'.

While describing Lord Shiva's proclamations to Kumara, sage Ribhu said that 'All is illusion', and continuing his discourse, Sage Ribhu elaborates upon that which is mithya i.e. unreal, not true, illusion and baseless. He specifically emphasized that Jivas (Jivatma or beings) comprehend the same (i.e. the world) as 'real and true' only out of 'Avidya' (i.e. ignorance).

In Srimad Bhagvatam (Chapter 2) Vidya and Avidya have been described thus:

The material body is the symbol of gross and subtle form of forgetfulness; therefore the whole atmosphere of the material world is call Avidya; whereas the whole atmosphere of the spiritual world is called Vidya.

It implies that the knowledge of universe is *Avidya* (ignorance), whereas the knowledge of Paramatma is *Vidya* (knowledge). It is so because human beings forget their real nature (of being a part of Paramatma, owing to their manifestation by the will of Paramatma) in this universe and thus fall prey to *Avidya*, while actual knowledge or *Vidya* consist in remembering one's real-Self.

In Devi Bhagavata Purana, Vidya and Avidya are explained as two opposing aspects of Maya (illusion) thus:

Vidya represents blissful intelligence, which promotes enlightenment and liberation; whereas Avidya represents ignorance and illusion, which creates obstacles and hides true-Self.

In Shiva Purana, *Vidya refers to consciousness or knowledge, while Avidya signifies insentience or ignorance.*

Some of the learned commentators, while explaining this Sloka of Isavasya Upanishad or the concepts of Vidya and Avidya have also said that *Vidya* refers to knowledge that leads to distinct results such as attainment of *Devaloka* (heaven) while *Avidya* represents ignorance or actions (*Karma*) that yield different outcomes depending on the *Karma*.

However, this explanation of *Vidya* is limiting in the sense that even *Devaloka* or heaven (a mental construct to signify the abode of Gods where there are only pleasures and no sorrows) isn't and can't be the final abode in spiritual terms. It is so because Gods aren't absolutely powerful, as *Paramatma* or Brahman is. Therefore, even the knowledge and subsequent Karmas leading a human being to *Devaloka* are only transient one and don't liberate a *Jivatma.*

(This aspect of 'Sambhuti' or those with absolute power and 'Asambhuti' i.e. those without absolute power are discussed in next chapter).

Therefore, only 'That' which liberates a being from the transmigratory cycle by knowing and experiencing oneness with *Paramatma* is *Vidya* and everything else is *Avidya.*

The second part of this sloka has highlighted the fact that only bookish knowledge and proud flaunting that knowledge to gain respect is even worse than mere ignorance.

It is so because for an ignorant human being, it is easier to start walking on the path of knowledge but for someone who has walked miles on the wrong path, he has to first return to point zero by accepting his egoistic tendencies (which is very hard for an egoistic person) and then start walking on the path of true knowledge.

This has also been highlighted in Srimadbhagvad Gita (16.4) wherein Shri Krishna has advised Arjun thus:

Pride, arrogance, conceit, anger and ignorance – these qualities belong to those of Asuri (demoniac) nature. Such beings want to make a show of their religious knowledge and advancement of spiritual pursuits, although they do not follow the principles. They are always arrogant or proud in possessing knowledge of the Vedas and Sastras. Though they desire to be respected and worshipped by others, yet ultimately they don't even get respect.

Further in Srimadbhagvad Gita (16.5-7), Shri Krishna has emphasized the fate of such demons thus:

The transcendental qualities are conducive to liberation, whereas demoniac qualities make for bondage. Those who are demoniac do not know what is to be done and what is not to be done. Neither cleanliness (of body, mind and intellect) nor proper behavior (as per Sastras) nor truth is found in them.

So, the essence of this Sloka of Isavasya Upanishad one should neither indulge in *Avidya*, nor one should feel egoistic attachment to one's scriptural knowledge and indulge in inappropriate behaviors involving pride, anger or ridiculing those who don't have scriptural or religious knowledge.

Sloka 10

This sloka has explained in a suggestive / symbolic language as to how one gets the best results by understanding the true meaning of scriptures and indulging-in or following the real and true knowledge i.e. *Jnana-Marg* and path of action i.e. *Karma-Marg.*

By following Vidya i.e. Jnana-Marg or path of true knowledge, one gets a different result (as compared to one explained in previous sloka which one gets by following Avidya); by following Karma-Marg (path of true action) one gets a different result; thus we have heard from the Dheer (steadfast and wise) beings, who have vividly explained this subject.

This sloka has suggested the following:

By following the real and true *Jnana-Marg* (knowledge-path), one gets the required discrimination (*Vivek*) between true and illusory, between real and unreal; one gets dispassion or indifference towards ephemeral, perishable, transient, worldly and other worldly pleasures and their means; one gets life full of restraint and purity and continuous contemplation of the only *Param-Brahman, Parameshwar or Paramatma.* This leads to realizing one's true Self (*Atma-Sakshatkar*) and its oneness with *Paramatma.*

This supreme result is not attainable by those who indulge in pride or ego-satisfaction by constantly thinking-of or displaying one's scriptural knowledge. Such ignorant beings get miserable results (ever stuck in transmigratory cycle of rebirth and consequent misery in this world) instead of the supreme result (*Moksha* or liberation by attaining oneness with *Paramatma*).

Similarly, the form of *Karma*, i.e. action, which imparts best and supreme results include:

Absence of sense of doership on the part of the being; absence of any expectation of results from any action; absence of attachment, anger and hatred; doing every action as per one's scriptural duty and according to situation; dedicating every action to the Almighty *Paramatma*, thereby considering oneself as an instrument of *Paramatma*.

By doing so, one is able to permanently get rid of one's *sanskaras* (mental imprints) and evil thoughts; and also get rid of the joys and sorrows related to worldly things, thereby stopping one's transmigratory cycle of rebirth.

Those beings who indulge in actions with a sense of doership and attachment get a different result and such beings get further entangled in the transmigratory cycle of birth and death.

In this way, *Dheer* i.e. the wise, self-restrained, steadfast, equanimous sages have explained both the paths (*Jnana and Karma*) separately.

These paths and results thereof are also described in great details in Srimadbhagvad Gita.

In Srimadbhagvad Gita (6.5) Shri Krishna declares that *'Elevate yourself through the power of your mind, and not degrade yourself; for the mind can be the friend and also the enemy of the Self'.*

This implies that a human being has to inspire oneself from within by taming one's mind and directing it towards the higher Self.

Further in Srimadbhagvad Gita (4.41), Shri Krishna says:

O Arjun, actions do not bind those who have renounced Karma in the fire of Yog (oneness with God), whose doubts have been dispelled by knowledge (vidya), and who are established in the knowledge of the Self (Atma).

And in the very next sloka of Srimadbhagvad Gita (4.42), Shri Krishna has advised Arjun thus:

Therefore, with the sword of knowledge (vidya), cut asunder the doubts that have arisen in your heart. O scion of Bharat, establish yourself in Karma Yog (Karma-path). Arise, stand up, and take action.

Thus, even in Srimadbhagvad Gita, wherein these two paths have been termed as *Jnana-Yog* and *Karma-Yog*, Bhagwan Shri Krishna has unequivocally emphasized the paths of *Jnana* and *Karma.*

Sloka 11

This sloka of Isavasya Upanishad has explained the essence of both *Jnana* (knowledge) and *Karma* (action) and their complementarity thus:

The being, who in true sense comes to know and understand the essence and real meaning of both i.e. Karma (action) and Jnana (knowledge) together, will be able to transcend death through Karma-Marg actions and through Jnana-Marg actions, he attains the nectar of Self-realization by being one with the eternal, blissful, indestructible Paramatma.

Of these two very important paths, *Karma-Marg* have been subsequently discussed in Brihadaranyaka Upanishad, Bhagvata Purana (11.20) and chapter 33 of Narada Purana. However, it has been discussed in detail in Srimadbhagvad Gita.

In chapter 3 of Srimadbhagvad Gita, Shri Krishna has strongly emphasized that '*those who have not yet reached the transcendental levels of spiritual development, i.e. become Jnani yogis, they should perform their duties/karmas as prescribed by scriptures*'.

Karma i.e. action has been further explained in detail in Srimadbhagvad Gita (4.16-17), wherein Shri Krishna advised Arjun (and thereby every human being) thus:

'What is action (karma) and what is inaction (akarma). Even the wise are confused in determining this. Now I shall explain to you the secret of Karma (action), by knowing which, you may free yourself from material bondage. You must understand the nature of all the three i.e. recommended action (karma), wrong action (vikarma) and inaction (akarma). The truth about these is profound and difficult to understand.'

Every activity that a human performs has been divided into three categories i.e.

- *Karma* (Action), which is auspicious action recommended by scriptures for regulating the senses and purifying the mind;
- *Vikarma* (forbidden action), which is inauspicious action prohibited by scriptures because they result in degradation of *Atma* (soul);
- *Akarm* (Inaction), which is an action performed without attachment to results i.e. merely for dedication to God and as a wish of God, by being a mere tool of God. *Akarm* i.e. inaction as described here doesn't have any karmic reactions or results and they don't entangle the soul further.

However, when it comes to performance or not performing *Karmas* (actions) and expectations thereof, the same has been explained in Srimadbhagvad Gita (2.47-49) thus:

Your work (action) is your responsibility, not its result. Never let the fruits of its actions be your motives, nor give-in to inaction i.e. lethargy or prohibited action. Set firmly in yourself, do your work without being attached to anything. Remain even-minded in success and failure. Even-mindedness is true yoga i.e. union with God.

This steadfastness, even-mindedness and non-attachment in every worldly activity performed by a being is what actually defines *Karma-Marg.*

This steadfastness and even-mindedness has been emphasized in Srimadbhagvad Gita (4.18) thus:

Those who see action in inaction and inaction in action are truly wise amongst humans. Although performing all kinds of actions, they are yogis and masters of their actions.

The below example from recent history helps make the *Karma-Marg* concept more clear.

King Chandragupta Maurya asked his mentor Chanakya – 'According to the Vedic scriptures, what is the role/position of king vis-à-vis his subjects?'

Chanakya replied – 'the king is the servant of the subjects of his kingdom and nothing more. His God-given duty is to help the citizens of his kingdom progress in their journey towards Self-realization i.e. attainment of God.'

This has also been highlighted in the very famous two slokas of Srimadbhagvad Gita (2.47-48) thus:

You have the right to perform your duties, but you are not entitled to the fruits of your actions. Never consider yourself to be the cause of the results of your actions, nor be attached to inaction. Be steadfast in the performance of your duty, abandoning attachment to success and failure. Such even-mindedness, equanimity is called Yog i.e. union with God.

Similarly *Jnana-Marg* (path of knowledge) has been described in Brihadaranyaka Upanishad (2.4.5) and in detail in Srimadbhagvad Gita.

In Srimadbhagvad Gita (2.55-59), state of the *jnani* has been described and it is similar to the *Jivanmukta* or *Videhmukta* state described earlier in Chapter 5:

Jnana is the discernment of or ability to discriminate between Purusha i.e. pure consciousness, as different from Prakriti i.e. matter and material. It is a path wherein one knows and realizes the unity between Self and the ultimate reality called Brahman or Parameshwar or Paramatma. A jnani or yogi or a transcendently situated is one who has discarded all selfish desires and cravings of the senses that torment the mind, and has become satisfied with Self-realization, which is realizing one's union with the God.

Apart from emphasizing the importance of *Jnana-Marg* and *Karma-Marg* in the lives of human beings, this very important sloka of *Isavasya Upanishad* has emphasized the complementary nature of both Karma and Jnana.

For a human being, it is not possible 'not to do' any action in this world. So, this sloka emphasizes that in order to transcend the transmigratory cycle of rebirth, one should start with performing actions as per scriptural guidance, in a completely detached manner, with a sense of duty, and without any expectations of results, thereof.

Subsequently, through perseverance on this path of *Karma* (inaction in action and action in inaction), one tends to realize the perishable and momentary nature of this world, its activities and one's own body.

This will lead to the intellect questioning: if everything that I see, hear, feel, think, associate with is temporary and destructible, then what is permanent, indestructible and eternal.

At this stage, *Jnana* i.e. knowledge path comes into play and through various steps of *Jnana-Marg*, one realizes one's true Self and its unity with the Paramatma.

Several subsequent scriptures have been written, exclusively focusing on each word or part of these 3 important slokas of the Isavasya Upanishad, because these 3 slokas are key to living one's life in this universe as well as attaining the final goal i.e. *Ekatva* or oneness with Paramatma.

How to proceed on these paths of *Karma* and *Jnana* have been detailed by sages through various steps, which one can follow to reach the ultimate supreme result i.e. Self-realization and realizing one's unity/oneness with *Paramatma*, thereby getting rid of the transmigratory cycle of rebirth and resulting sorrows and miseries of life. For example:

- In Srimadbhagvad Gita, the life path for a being has been described by Shri Krishna through *Jnana-Yog, Karma-Yog, Bhakti-Yog* and *Raja-Yog*.
- In Ribhu Gita, it has been emphasized by sage Ribhu at every step, in every chapter, as to how every action is Brahman itself and how only *Brahman* is real, while everything else is illusion.
- In Yoga-Sutras, sage Patanjali has given steps for Self-realization through Yoga and meditation.
- In Vivekachudamani, sage Adi Shankaracharya has given detailed steps for developing discrimination (*Vivek*) that results in realizing the difference between real (*Paramatma*) and unreal (this universe

and a being's body, mind, intellect and related attributes).

Thus, a human being needs to understand the essence and real meaning of *Vidya* and *Avidya*, and then also understand true purport and significance of *Jnana* and *Karma* and then live one's life in such a way that he is able to get rid of the miseries and sorrow of this earthly life through stopping one's transmigratory cycle of rebirth and then attain oneness with *Paramatma*, which the supreme goal of every being.

AUM TAT SAT AUM

*****

7. Absolute Power

The next 3 slokas of Isavasya Upanishad, i.e. 12th, 13th and 14th, describe the essence and true meaning of '*Sambhuti*' (one with absolute power) and '*Asambhuti*' (one without absolute power).

Further, these slokas have described that having understood the real meaning and difference between the two, how one should utilize the knowledge and act for one's liberation from the transmigratory cycle of birth and death and attain oneness with *Paramatma*.

'*Sambhuti*' or the 'one with absolute power' is none other than the supreme *Brahman*, which is variously named as *Parameshwar* or *Ishwar* or *Paramatma*; whereas '*Asambhuti*' or those 'without absolute power' are the Gods, Gurus, ancestors or saints/sages or various temporary constructs of universe, which may be very powerful but do not have the absolute power, because absolute power resides only in *Paramatma*.

Though both *Paramatma* (i.e. the One with absolute power) or '*Sambhuti*' as well as Gods, Saints, Gurus, ancestors etc. (i.e. those who are/may be very powerful but without absolute power) or '*Asambhuti*' are worshipped by the human beings, yet it is important and essential to understand them and accordingly (i.e. according to the understanding of the essence of both concepts) worship Paramatma as well as those without absolute power, for the supreme result.

To understand the purport or essence of this, the next sloka i.e. 12th sloka describes the miseries suffered by those who worship *Sambhuti* or *Asambhuti*, without understanding the real meaning of the same.

Sloka 12

Those human beings who worship Asambhuti (i.e. Devtas or Gods, Saints, Gurus, Ancestors etc.) are destined to go into the darkest alleys of ignorance; and those who worship Sambhuti (i.e. Paramatma, Parameshwar or Brahman which is/have the absolute power) with a feeling of indulgence, obsession and delusional pride, they go to even more dark alleys of ignorance.

The purport of the first part of this sloka is:

Those human beings who consider worldly pleasures i.e. physical gratifications, wealth, powerful positions or designations, fame etc. as the real pleasures and remain attached to the world and beyond; and not only keep accumulating materialistic assets but also keep praying *Sambhuti* (i.e. Gods, Saints, Gurus or Ancestors) for getting access to or accumulation of these worldly things, are certain to keep themselves entangled in the vicious cycle of transmigration i.e. birth-death cycle repeating itself with no end in sight. These repeating cycle of birth-death in this world full of miseries, sorrow, pleasures and pains etc. which are referred to as the darkest alleys of ignorance.

In Srimadbhagvad Gita chapter 7, verses 20, 22 and 23, Shri Krishna has advised Arjun thus:

Those whose knowledge has been veiled by material world, surrender to celestial Gods and following their ignorant nature, they worship the Devtas to attain material desires.

Endowed with faith, the devotee worships a particular celestial God and obtains the objects of desire. But the fruit/result generated by these persons of little understanding, is perishable (like the entire universe is).

Those who worship the celestial Gods go to celestial abodes like heaven, while those who worship Me (i.e. Paramatma) come to Me.

In the above slokas, Shri Krishna too has advised Arjun (and to every human being) that worshipping *Asambhuti* (Devtas, celestial Gods etc.) can only get worldly desires fulfilled but can't provide the Supreme fruit or result, which is realizing

Paramatma and one's unity with 'Him', thereby ensuring end of one's rebirth cycle.

The purport of the second part of this sloka of *Isavasya Upanishad* is:

Apart from the devotees described in first part, there are others who keep worshipping *Paramatma* outwardly without truly knowing 'Him' and keep seeking worldly pleasures in return. They remain under the illusion that they are worshipping *Parameshwar* and feel proud of the same, taking themselves to be higher mortals. Such ignorant people also stop respecting the learned saints, sacred scriptures, even some Gods, Gurus and their brethren.

Such delusional human beings are even worse than the first category because they are committing fraud in the name of Paramatma and therefore such people are holding on to an even bigger illusion, about themselves, about *Sambhuti* and about knowledge per se.

Therefore, their chances of returning to the real path of knowledge and truth and path to *Ekatva* with *Paramatma* are very remote and that's why in this sloka, such people have been categorized as the ones stuck in even darker than the darkest alleys of ignorance.

In Srimadbhagvad Gita (16. 18-19), such people and their fates have been described by Shri Krishna thus:

Blinded by ego, strength, anger, desire and arrogance, the demonic nature people abuse Me (Paramatma as well as everyone else who is manifestation of Paramatma only), whereas I (Paramatma) am present in their own body as well as in the bodies of others.

These vile, arrogant, cruel and hateful persons, I constantly hurl into the wombs of those with similar demoniac nature in the cycle of rebirth, in the material world. These ignorant should take birth again and again. Failing to attain Me (i.e. Paramatma), they gradually sink to the most abominable types of existence.

Sloka 3 of chapter 11 of Srimadbhagvad Gita has summed-up the fate of those who are under the pale of ignorance thus:

Those who act under the impulse of desire, discarding the injunctions of scriptures, attain neither perfection and nor happiness in this world, nor do they get the supreme goal of life i.e. Self-realization and attaining Paramatma, thereby end of rebirth cycle.

Having described the miseries of the disillusioned or misguided people, who don't understand the true and real meaning of *Sambhuti* and *Asambhuti* and keep worshipping as per their materialistic desires and illusions, the next sloka of *Isavasya Upanishad*, i.e. Sloka 13, has suggested about those who understand Sastras i.e. sacred scriptures and the true meanings, essence and purport of *Sambhuti* and *Asambhuti* and then accordingly worship *Paramatma* or *devtas* i.e. celestial Gods, Saints, Gurus and Ancestors.

Sloka 13

By worshipping indestructible, eternal Brahman, one gets a different result; by worshipping perishable or non-eternal Gods-Saints/Gurus-Ancestors etc., one get different results. This is what we have heard from the Dheer (steadfast, equanimous wise men i.e. the Self-realized ones), who have explained this subject to us very well.

The real form of worship of *Param-Brahman Parameshwar* is knowing, understanding and assimilating *Paramatma* as the Supreme Power (*sarvocch-satta*), omnipotent (*sarv-shaktiman*), omnipresent (*sarvbhoot*), omniscient (*sarvgya*), who supports all (*sarvadhar*), pervading everything everywhere (*sarv-vyapt*).

Having known *Paramatma* as such, one must contemplate on 'Him' with utmost devotion, love, belief, faith and reverence. By doing so, one attains oneness or unity with 'Him', which is the supreme result that the first part of this sloka has indicated about.

In Srimadbhagvad Gita (9.34), Shri Krishna has said the same thus:

Always think of Me (i.e. Paramatma), be devoted to Me, worship Me, and offer obeisance to Me. Once you have dedicated your mind and body to Me, you will certainly come to Me.

Worshipping *Paramatma* isn't about external actions but it is about Knowing Him truly and then continuously contemplating about Paramatma, with full devotion, belief and faith.

Those persons who falsely and arrogantly pose as worshippers, without understanding the true meaning of *Parameshwar* and keep pretending and posing as worshippers, tend to get a miserable result, which is not the supreme result (described above) for the true humble worshippers of *Parameshwar.*

This sloka of *Isavasya Upanishad* further indicates that those who worship Gods, Saints, Gurus, and Ancestors etc. with worldly desires don't get the supreme results, which true humble worshippers of *Paramatma* get blessed in the form of *Atma-sakshatkar* i.e. Self-realization and *Moksha* i.e. liberation by attaining *Ekatva* (oneness) with Paramatma.

Human beings generally worship Devtas, Gods, Gurus, and Saints etc. for worldly pleasures and materialistic desires and may get fulfilment of the same too, but this results in further entanglement of such persons in the rebirth cycle, so how can they get the supreme result of worship.

Srimadbhagvad Gita (17.14) describe the same essence as below:

One must worship devtas, ancestors, and gurus, parents (i.e. Asambhuti or the ones without absolute power) as forms of Paramatma, follow their advice obediently as one's duty, but 'without any desire of results (nishkam bhav)' and as supreme service to Paramatma. By doing so, one's conscience becomes pure and one is bestowed with the blessings of Paramatma. Thus, one gets liberated from the clutches of the vicious transmigratory cycle of rebirth.

In Ribhu Gita, sage Ribhu has emphasized that *only Brahman is real and any tarpan (i.e. the daily water offering or libation or ablution, which is a common practice among religious Hindus) to ancestors, homa (i.e. fire-sacrifice or oblation) to deities, worship of any devta or of the Guru should only be with the understanding that all the devtas, deities, ancestors, gurus are forms of Brahman alone.*

Sage Ribhu has further emphasized that *one should abide in the certitude that - Death, physical pleasures, heaven and hell, and the world of cardinal directions are all illusory, being fabrications by the mind itself. I am Brahman alone, without doubt. Thus, one should only contemplate on Brahman or Paramatma.*

Going even a step further, sage Ribhu advised his disciple Nidagha that *Forbearance, deep meditation, earnestness, utterance of a teacher, the longing for liberation, the ideal of living for moksha (liberation) – are all said to be bondage. So, effectively he has said that even the desire for liberation from the transmigratory cycle is a bondage and must be done away with and one must only contemplate on Brahman (i.e. Paramatma) without any desires whatsoever.*

As per 'The Gospel of The Holy Mother; page 87', in more recent times (in 1909), when a disciple asked the revered saint Sri Sharada Maa about importance of *japa* (constant repeatition of God's name) and other spiritual practices, She replied thus:

"Through these spiritual disciplines, the ties of past karma are cut asunder. Do you know the significance of japa and other spiritual practices? By these the dominance of sense organs is subdued."

Further, continuing his reply to the disciple, The Holy Mother has explained that:

"But realization of God (meaning Paramatma) cannot be achieved without ecstatic love (param-bhakti) for Paramatma."

The significance of understanding the meanings of both *Sambhuti* and *Asambhuti* and how to worship both aspects (as also told by the Holy Mother Sri Sharada Maa) for attaining supreme result, have been explained in the next sloka of the Isavasya Upanishad.

Sloka 14

Those human beings who know, understand and assimilate the true meaning of Sambhuti (i.e. the absolutely powerful Paramatma) and Asambhuti (i.e. those without absolute power such as devtas, saints, gurus, ancestors etc.) simultaneously, they reach beyond death through worshipping the devtas etc. and attain the supreme nectar (attain oneness with Paramatma) through worshipping the Paramatma.

This sloka has described the meaning of true worship and complementarity of worshipping Sambhuti and Asambhuti to achieve the supreme fruit.

One must know, understand and assimilate that *Sambhuti* (i.e. *Param-Brahman Parameshwar*) is eternal, indestructible, pervading everywhere, omnipotent, omnipresent, omniscient, supporting everything, universal soul (*sarv-Atma*), and the Supreme One; and that *Parameshwar* is with as well as without attributes, and 'He' is beyond the beyond.

One must also understands that all the *Asambhuti* (i.e. *devtas,* saints, *gurus,* ancestors) and their various forms and pleasures as well as results provided by them (except guiding towards Paramatma) are reasons for miseries and sorrows because they are all destructible, impermanent, momentary and destined for end or death.

Such a one, who has known the above, will not desire and get attached to the worldly pleasures and fulfilment of worldly desires through the worship of the *Asambhuti*; but he will worship (as per scriptural guidance) the *Asambhuti* without any attachment and expectation of results. By doing so such a person gets detached from body and worldly attachments, thereby cutting ties of *karma* asunder.

Having moved to this state of purity of mind, when that person worships *Paramatma* wholeheartedly through utmost devotion, love, faith and perseverance, he attains self-realization and oneness or union (*Ekatva*) with *Paramatma.*

If we take the teachings of *Karma-Marg* and *Jnana-Marg* and then understand *Sambhuti* and *Asambhuti* together with *Karma-Marg* and *Jnana-Marg,* then it becomes easier to understand that these slokas of the Isavasya Upanishad are guiding us to worship *Asambhuti* through *Karma-Marg* or *Karma-Yog,* and worship *Sambhuti* through *Jnana-Marg* or *Jnana-Yog.*

Thus, till now Isavasya Upanishad has attempted to guide human beings through their lives and how to proceed with the same for the supreme result i.e. attainment of oneness (*Ekatva*) with *Paramatma*, which the real purpose of every *Jivatma*.

Several sacred scriptures, sacred texts and religious books have the essence and wisdom of Isavasya Upanishad as the basis and have built upon these basic spiritual slokas.

AUM TAT SAT AUM

*****

8. Final Prayer

Till now, in the last 14 slokas of *Isavasya Upanishad*, it has been said that knowing and then worshipping *Paramatma* through continuous contemplation, utmost devotion and infinite faith and love for 'Him' and 'His' creation, and perseverance on this path, one achieves the ultimate Grace of *Paramatma* i.e. Self-Realization and '*Ekatva*' (union) with 'Him'.

However, till one (*Jivatma*) has this body and it's *Prarabdha* (destiny) to continue on the earthly plane, one has to continue his assigned work, though one must do so without a sense of doership, and with every thought and activity being an offering to the Parameshwar.

But, whatever is born will eventually die, so *Jivatma* too will shed this body as per its destiny.

The next two slokas i.e. sloka 15 and 16 describe as to what it is that one must pray to the *Paramatma* before shedding this perishable, impermanent and temporary body i.e. what must one pray to *Paramatma* before death.

Sloka 15

O Paramatma! Provider, nurturer and sustainer of all, the true Self! Your real Self is hidden behind the dazzling effulgence; kindly remove this veil / mantle, so that I, who devotionally worships you by following true / real path i.e. Satvik-Marg, can have your Darshan (i.e. auspicious vision of Paramatma).

In this sloka, the devotee or the seeker, who has been trudging on the *Satvik* (righteous) path and worshipping *Paramatma* after truly knowing and understanding 'Him', desires and prays to have a vision of *Param-Brahman Parameshwar.*

But he is dazzled by the effulgence of purity and aura of countenance of the Omnipotent and Supremely Blissful *Paramatma.* Therefore, the seeker is humbly and devotedly praying the *Paramatma* to let him have 'His' *Darshan* i.e. vision or experience.

A few very important aspects have been brought-forward and emphasized in this sloka, i.e.:

Firstly, the seeker has assimilated the true meaning i.e. essence of *Parameshwar* and that 'He' is the only sustainer of everyone and this whole universe and beyond.

Secondly, Parameshwar is so effulgent that 'His' vision is beyond ordinary senses of human beings.

Thirdly, 'His' vision can only be possible through 'His' Grace and Blessings, so one needs to pray and worship 'Him' for 'His' Grace.

Fourth, only by following or treading on a *Satvik* path i.e. a path of truth and purity and through devotion, love and faith for 'Him' and 'His' creation, one can have a vision or attain *Paramatma*.

In some slokas, the word 'Dheer' has been used saying – 'so was told to us by the Dheer Purusha'. We have used the words wise, steadfast and equanimous to explain this word. In Srimadbhagvad Gita (11.15), *Dheer Purusha* has been explained thus:

That man whom these (worldly conditions such as pain-pleasure or heat-cold or success-defeat or fame – disrespect etc.) torments not, balanced in pain and pleasure, steadfast, he is fit for immortality.

To explain it further, it refers to those steadfast, balanced minded, equanimous, wise people who don't get affected by varying aspects of worldly life but remain totally unaffected and steadfast, without any reactions whatsoever.

This demeanour isn't an outside mask of such people but through continuous meditation and sadhna, they have calmed their mind and intellect. Such people are the ones who are ready to progress on the path of *Ekatva* (oneness) with *Paramatma*. Several sages have walked this earth since times immemorial and are still doing so with this state of their body, mind and intellect.

Sloka 16

O sustainer of devotees, supreme form of knowledge, regulator (i.e. controller and restrainer) of all; the ultimate goal of all the wise seekers, divine goal of Prajapati (God Brahma); (I pray to you to) kindly either remove the dazzling rays of Your effulgence or remove the effulgent aura of Your divinity, (so that) I can see (i.e. experience) your divine form. With Your kind Grace, through meditation I am able to visualize 'That' (soul of the Sun), the Supreme Soul (which is your form) and I am also 'That'.

This sloka of Isavasya Upanishad has highlighted the below:

Having aptly propitiated and spoken of the glories of *Paramatma*, the wise, steadfast men (*dheer purush*) humbly prays and begs the Almighty *Paramatma* to shower 'His' benediction and blessings on 'His' devotee by making 'His' Self visible (to the earthly seeker with limited capabilities) by either removing the dazzling rays (which can't be seen towards by the limited sensory capabilities of human eyes) or allow the devotee to have 'His' vision by inwardly enfolding 'His' effulgent aura, so that the devotee is able to see, visualize and experience the serene, peaceful, purest and supremely blissful *Paramatma*.

During *Gita-Upadesh*, Arjun prays Shri Krishna for vision of his actual form. When Shri Krishna gracefully agrees to Arjun's prayer and reveals 'His' cosmic form, Arjun is completely dazzled.

On being completely dazzled by 'His' effulgent, dazzling, unlimited and primeval cosmic form vision, Arjun also had to request Shri Krishna to return to 'His' humanly form, as having a vision and comprehending 'His' cosmic form was beyond the capabilities of Arjun's senses. Mind and intellect.

This 16th sloka of *Isavasya Upanishad* also highlights that any experience or vision of Paramatma is possible only by the Grace and blessings of the *Paramatma*.

In Srimadbhagvad Gita (11.47-48), it has been explained thus:

Shri Krishna said, Arjun being pleased with you, I gave you a vision of My resplendent, effulgent, unlimited, primeval cosmic form. No one before you has ever seen it. No mortal can ever see 'It' by study of Vedas, nor by performance of sacrifices, rituals or charity, not even by practicing severe austerities.

This (i.e. vision or experience of Paramatma) is what the devotee is desirous of visualizing / experiencing before death, in this sloka.

It is so because on receiving 'His' divine vision, one realizes one's *Ekatva* (union or oneness) with 'Him'.

Even Shri Krishna has alluded to the same viewpoint in Srimadbhagvad Gita (11.52, 54, and 55) thus:

This form of Mine that you are seeing is exceedingly difficult to behold. Even the celestial Gods are eager to see It. O Arjun, by pure devotion alone can I be known as I am, standing before you. Thereafter, on receiving My divine vision, one can enter into union with Me.

Those who perform all their duties for My sake, who depend upon Me and are entirely devoted to Me, who are free from attachment, and are without malice towards all beings, such devotees certainly come to Me.

The wise devotee thus prays to and requests Paramatma to bless the devotee by 'His' experience / vision. Further he expresses his contemplated knowledge by asserting that he (i.e. devotee) knows that he himself (as individual soul or *Jivatma*) and *Paramatma* (Universal Soul) are one only and that this blessing of *Paramatma*, in the form of letting the devotee have a *Paramatmic* experience, will solidify devotee's contemplated truth.

The 15th and 16th slokas of Isavasya Upanishad are beneficial for everyone, at whatever spiritual stage or life stage one may be.

A seeker / devotee must always meditate and contemplate on the *Paramatma*, by assimilating 'His' supreme power in every aspect of known and unknown sphere.

In addition to this, meditation and contemplation on Paramatma, one must be a truthful and pure devotee (Bhakta), always seeking / praying for 'His' mercy in the form of Self-Realization and Ekatva (union) with Paramatma, in this life itself.

These two slokas also emphasize the complementarity of *Jnana-Marg* (path of knowledge) and *Bhakti-Marg* (path of devotion).

AUM TAT SAT AUM

*****

9. State of a Mumurshu

After *Darshan* (visualization i.e. experience) of the auspicious and supremely blissful form of the *Paramatma*, the seeker / devotee is now anxious and eager to reach / merge with (*Ekatva*) with *Paramatma*, by shedding his physical body.

The last and next two slokas of the *Isavasya Upanishad*, i.e. sloka 17th and 18th, describe the state of a *Mumurshu* (i.e. a seeker just before death).

Sloka 17

Now let the Prana and its related senses enter / merge with the immortal and total air element; let this physical body end itself in the fire element; O Sacchidanand (Existence-Consciousness-Bliss i.e. Paramatma), Lord of sacrifice, (I pray to you to) kindly remember me, kindly remember all the actions performed by me.

The devotee, the seeker, the traveller of the final journey towards the supremely blissful abode of *Paramatma*, has realized his separateness from his body, mind and intellect i.e. he has realized that he himself is the eternal, indestructible *Atma* (soul) and not this body of his (as he has been presuming his whole life on earthly plane).

Therefore, this enlightened, Self-realized *Jivatma* wishes to let the *Panchbhutas* (five elements constituting body as well as all the cosmic creation i.e. this universe and they are earth, water, fire, air and Akash or ether) merge with the total *bhautik tattvas* (physical elements of their class forming the entire universe).

He has realized that the *Prana* (life-giving air that he has been inhaling and exhaling and which was responsible for continuity of his physical existence on earth) is only a part of universal air element, which in turn is a creation of *Paramatma.*

The devotee now wishes to annihilate his physical existence, as he has realized that his physical time on earthly plane is close to its end and he has also realized the futility of its existence, any longer.

Therefore, he prays to the *Paramatma* to remember him (i.e. the devotee) and he repeats his prayer to the Paramatma to remember him and his works. Why does he do that?

The answer to this comes from *Varaha Purana*, wherein *Paramatma* (being referred to as *Sri Hari* or *Bhagwan Krishna*) has been called '*Satkriti*', meaning the one who helps 'His' devotees during the devotee's last moments of physical existence.

In the slokas of Varaha Purana, it is mentioned that *'If a true and pure devotee isn't able to remember 'Me' (i.e. Paramatma) during his last moments, even then, 'I' (i.e. Paramatma), remembers the devotee to provide him liberation (Param-Gati or Moksha)'.*

The devotee is aware of this blessing of *Paramatma* and therefore, he not only prays to the Paramatma to remember him i.e. the devotee, but also repeats his prayer. He sincerely wishes to get liberated from this transmigratory cycle of rebirth. He is assured of the fact that if *Paramatma* 'Himself' remembers the devotee, then liberation is a certainty.

In Srimadbhagvad Gita (8.10), it is clearly stated thus:

One who, at the time of death, fixes his life air between the eyebrows, and by the strength of Yoga, engages himself in remembering the Paramatma with full devotion, will certainly 'attain to' the Supreme Paramatma.

Further in Srimadbhagvad Gita (8.15), Shri Krishna says thus:

After attaining Me, the sincere, faithful, true and pure Yogis, never return to this temporary world, which is full of miseries; because they have attained the highest perfection.

This sloka has spelled-out in very clear terms as to what does 'attaining Paramatma' mean and why this is the highest goal of every human being in this universe.

After this prayer (as given in sloka 17), the devotee prays to the *Agni-devta* (fire-element of Paramatma) and the same is explained in next sloka.

Sloka 18

O Agni-devta (i.e. the Presiding deity of the fire-element)! (I pray to you to) please carry me to the supremely blissful, serene and peaceful abode of the Paramatma, kindly take me through the auspicious path; O God! You know all my Karmas (deeds), therefore, all those sinful Karmas of mine which can be a hindrance, I pray to you to kindly remove them. I pray you, I pray you again and again.

In this last sloka of Isavasya Upanishad, the devotee is praying to the *Agni-Devta* (supreme deity of the fire element). But why Agni-Devta?

In Rig-Veda, Agni is called the "first-born of creation" and represents the pure and primordial energy of the universe. In the very first sloka of Rig-Veda (1.1), Agni is invoked as the priest of the Yajna. It means whatever is given to (Arpan) Agni by invoking any particular Deity, reached that deity.

So, Agni is the divine power that connects all the other divine powers. At the same time, *Rig-Veda (1.1.5) spells out different qualities of Agni as being far-sighted with wisdom, embodiment of truth and one who is uniquely famed.*

Being the divine power which connects all other divine powers, *Agni* is associated with funeral pyres in *Hinduism*. It is believed that *Agni* leads the dead to their final destination.

Since the perishable body gets burned down, what is it that the Agni-Devta leads to his final destination? It is *Jivatma* (also termed as soul), which is eternal, indestructible and permanent which is carried by the *Agni-Devta*.

Here the devotee prays to the Agni-Devta to take him to the *Param-Dham* (i.e. auspicious abode) of the *Paramatma*.

Neither *Paramatma*, nor *Jivatma* nor *Param-Dham* are physical entities and therefore they are beyond the grasp of our senses, mind or intellect. However, when one experiences his real Self (i.e. Atma-Sakshatkar), and becomes Self-Realized, it is very easy to understand.

Being consciously aware of the fact that the devotee's sinful deeds (if any) may act as hindrance to his entry into the *Param-Dham* of *Paramatma* i.e. his union with *Paramatma*; he prays the *Agni-Devta* to destroy all his sinful *Karmas*, as *Agni* (being the epitome of wisdom) is very much aware of such Karmas on part of the devotee. Also, fire is said to be the ultimate destroyer, which has a capacity to destroy everything, so the devotee is requesting *Agni-Devta* to burn and destroy all his sinful deeds.

He is repeating his prayer again and again, as he is very anxious to have union (*Ekatva*) with *Paramatma*, which will ensure his liberation from the transmigratory rebirth cycle of birth, death and miseries and sorrows of the worldly life.

These last two slokas are very important for a devotee during his final moments before death.

Now, no one knows when that moment will come in one's lifetime, and that is why all the sacred scriptures, including Vedas and Upanishads, emphasize constantly remembering the supremely benevolent *Paramatma*, at every moment of one's life on this earth.

The best approach to do will be remember 'Him', contemplate on 'Him', dedicate every thought/motive/action to 'Him', love 'Him', remain devoted to 'Him' and have complete faith in 'Him'.

This has also been echoed by Shri Krishna in Srimadbhagvad Gita (8.7) thus:

Therefore, always remember Me and do your duty of fighting the war. With mind and intellect surrendered to Me, you will definitely attain Me; of this, there is no doubt.

Here Shri Krishna advises Arjun to do his assigned *Karma* i.e. fighting the war; but even in such an intense earthly *Karma* of fighting a war, Arjun is being advised to remember Paramatma. This is a universal message for every human being, irrespective of profession, location and time.

AUM TAT SAT AUM

AUM SHANTI SHANTI SHANTI

*****

Epilogue

Though *Isavasya Upanishad* is the smallest *Upanishad*, yet it contains the essence of the Vedic philosophy and remain one of the most profound teaching for every human being.

Several subsequent Upanishads, Srimadbhagvad Gita and numerous other scriptures by eminent saints such as Adi Shankaracharya have further built upon, expanded and explained the concepts or the teachings of Isavasya Upanishad including universality, eternal nature, indestructibility of Paramatma and various paths for attaining union (Ekatva) with Paramatma.

May you attain the final goal of every human being, every seeker and devotee i.e. *Atma-Sakshatkar* (i.e. Self-Realization) and *Moksha* (i.e. liberation from transmigratory cycle of rebirth) through final *Ekatva* (union) with the *Paramatma*.

AUM TAT SAT AUM

AUM SHANTI SHANTI SHANTIH

About Raj Bhambu

Raj Bhambu has donned various hats i.e. of being an Indian Army Officer, a Banker, and Corporate Leader in MNCs, an Entrepreneur, Strategy Consultant and an Author.

Raj has always been a spiritual person and an avid reader. He has co-authored 04 books with his sister Anshu Chaudhary:

1. And We Worked Happily Ever after
2. You @ Your Best
3. Work-Life Mantras
4. Shiva Jnana

Subsequently, he has also authored 'Teachings of The Ribhu Gita'.

Raj to the readers, devotees, seekers:

"If this commentary on Isavasya Upanishad hasn't been upto your expectations, then I seek sincere apology and forgiveness. Being an *Alpagya* (ignorant) seeker myself, I am trying to walk on this path earnestly. We are all on a journey, hoping to improve our knowledge about 'Him' through various means and this is one of them.

May Paramatma Bless You always !!!

www.ingramcontent.com/pod-product-compliance
Lightning Source LLC
LaVergne TN
LVHW091111150826
845673LV00002B/777

* 9 7 9 8 8 9 7 4 4 4 5 9 5 *